a day with the Lord

VOLUME I
ADVENT AND CHRISTMASTIDE

W9-CJP-679

a day with the Lord

VOLUME I
ADVENT AND CHRISTMASTIDE

Rev. John A. Crowley

Our Sunday Visitor Publishing Division
Our Sunday Visitor, Inc.
Huntington, Indiana 46750

Copyright © 1990
by Our Sunday Visitor Publishing Division
Our Sunday Visitor, Inc.
ALL RIGHTS RESERVED

With the exception of short excerpts for critical reviews, no part
of this book may be reproduced or transmitted in any form or by any
means, electronic or mechanical, including photocopying, recording,
or by any information storage or retrieval system, without permission
in writing from the publisher. *Write:*
Our Sunday Visitor Publishing Division
Our Sunday Visitor, Inc.
200 Noll Plaza
Huntington, Indiana 46750

International Standard Book Number: 0-87973-471-X
Library of Congress Catalog Card Number: 90-60645

PRINTED IN THE UNITED STATES OF AMERICA

Cover design by James E. McIlrath

471

To
Mary, Mother of Priests

Preface

After returning from missionary work in Central America, I was assigned to St. John Vianney College Seminary in Miami in 1967. Seminary work was to be my assignment for the next sixteen years. Five of these years were spent at the minor seminary in Miami, and eleven of them were spent at the major seminary of St. Vincent de Paul at Boynton Beach.

During my tenure in the seminary, I taught Spanish, English, and Latin American Studies. Being director of St. Vincent de Paul Seminary Library also fell to my lot.

Seminary professors do not have to preach every day; they take their turn, and a good week or more might intervene before they mount the pulpit again. Not until my assignment to a parish church in West Palm Beach did I realize what a challenge preaching every day on the daily Gospel really was.

The Second Vatican Council stressed the importance of proclaiming the Word of God, and urged that it be done every day. I did just that, and found myself delving into my files, Scripture commentaries, and the spiritual classics in order to give the people a good solid talk for the day.

At first, I simply threw these little homilies away. Later I realized that perhaps other priests and ministers might profit from all the work I poured into this homily preparation. The thought also occurred to me that perhaps the laity could use these homilies as a meditative help and guide for their daily reflection on the Gospel message for each day. With that in mind I began to save them and put them into computer files in 1985.

These sermons are a product of years of reading and reflection. The plan I adopted was to both make this work a versatile tool in the hands of the homilist and a good meditative aid to the average lay person.

From the Gospel situation and milieu, I strove to weave the Gospel into our everyday life situation, draw a practical spiritual and moral lesson from it, and apply it to modern life. There are many sermon-illustration stories to help make the Gospel applicable to modern-day life.

These talks are structured into major and minor divisions. They are placed accordingly under both Roman and Arabic numerals. This is principally for the benefit of the homilist, who at any time can eliminate some of the points of the homily, add his own, and still maintain a unified and coherent talk. It has the built-in advantage of being able to be used in its entirety or to be modified by the homilist at will.

Each homily is accompanied by a series of petitions which are in harmony with the theme of the Gospel of that day. The homilists pick out one point from the Gospel and develop that point, so that the lesson taken from the Gospel is maintained throughout the talk.

Included in this work will be an extensive subject and biblical index (to be published as a separate volume). It will serve to put a given subject into the Gospel *Sitz in Leben* or milieu and enable the homilist to work out from a scriptural setting.

Hopefully, those who use this work might find it a real asset, a positive meditative aid, and a supple tool, especially in the area of the daily homily.

Rev. John A. Crowley
February 25, 1990
St. John of the Cross Parish, Vero Beach, Fla.

ADVENT

Monday, First Week of Advent: Mt. 8:5-11

I. Jews were not permitted to enter into the homes of the Gentiles nor even to speak with them. The Roman centurion realized this; nevertheless, he was so confident in the mercy and compassion of Jesus that he dared to approach Him and ask that He cure his servant. He had heard that Jesus had spoken to and cured sinners, publicans, and outcasts, such as the lepers and tax collectors. Realizing that he had broken one of the Jewish rules by conversing with a Jew, the centurion felt that he should not add to his audacity by asking Jesus to come to his house to lay hands on his servant.

II. Jesus was completely taken by the centurion's faith and confidence in Him and said, "I assure you, I have never found this much faith in Israel."

1) Jesus warns the Jews who think that their salvation is secure because they are sons and daughters of Abraham in the flesh and therefore a chosen people. Jesus says to them: "Many will come from the East and the West and will find a place at the banquet in the kingdom of God with Abraham, Isaac, and Jacob."

2) Faith in Our Lord Jesus Christ would be the only passport to heaven now, and the centurion possessed it while many of the Jewish onlookers did not.

III. Faith is a gift of God, and without it, says St. Paul, it is impossible to please God.

1) So pleased is Our Lord with our faith, confidence, and trust in His Providence that He confided to St. Gertrude the Great: "Though I look with kindness on all that is done for My glory, like prayers, fasts, and acts of piety, yet the confidence with which My elect have recourse to Me touches Me still more deeply" (Rodriguez, *Practice of Perfection and the Christian Virtues*).

2) In her *Dialogues*, St. Catherine of Siena writes of the words that Our Lord spoke to her: "The more you abandon yourself to Me and trust in Me, the more I will console you with My grace and make you feel My presence."

3) St. Francis de Sales writes, "We must trust fully in God, and the more lively and perfect our confidence in Him is, the more will the Lord have a special Providence over us" (*The Spiritual Conferences of St. Francis de Sales*).

4) "Even though things do not turn out as we should like," says

11

St. Vincent de Paul, "let us never doubt that Providence will arrange everything to our greatest good" (Maynard, *The Virtues and Doctrine of St. Vincent de Paul).*

5) Such was the confident trust that St. Ignatius Loyola had in God that he said he was prepared to thrust himself to the deep in an oarless, sailless skiff in complete abandonment to God's Providence.

6) The confidence and trust of the centurion in Our Lord Jesus Christ was daring. St. Bernard says that confidence is successful to the degree that it is daring in its hope.

7) Mother Teresa was offered half a million dollars, but it had one string attached: she would have to invest it, and with the interest earned provide security for her sisters. She declined, thinking that it would be an affront to Divine Providence and trust in God's goodness.

IV. John Wesley, the founder of the Methodist denomination, was once in the throes of a storm on the Atlantic while making his journey to America. He was terrified, yet he saw others maintaining a confident tranquillity. Wesley was impressed and wanted to know the secret of such faith in God. He realized that he did not possess such trust. He was told to "act as if you do have such faith and in time faith of that nature will take hold of you." Wesley followed this advice, and developed a deep trust and confidence in God that enabled him to pass through many difficulties in later years. Indeed, psychologist William James called this attitude an "as if" principle. He maintained that if you want a certain quality, act as if you already possess it; it will grow on you (*Pulpit Resource*).

1) If Jesus commanded us to pray, our prayers would be in vain if this command were empty. If the Lord wants us to pray, it is precisely because He means to answer our prayers. We must act as if we are going to get it.

2) Jesus gives us His word, and that is our guarantee: "Whatsoever you ask in prayer, believe that you will receive it, and you will" (Mk. 11:24).

****

1) That the Lord bless us with a lively confidence in our prayers.
2) That we come to trust more and more in His Providence.
3) That the Lord bless us with a deep and vibrant faith.

4) That we be not discouraged in our prayers, knowing that the Lord is wont to try our faith and test our confidence in Him.

5) That we persist in asking and not give up.

6) That we be compassionate and sensitive to the needs of others.

Tuesday, First Week of Advent: Lk.10:21-24

I. Faith is a pure gift of God. It is given to children as well as adults. It is not the exclusive property of brilliant minds; indeed, many brilliant people with university training have little or no faith.

II. The heart rather than the head is the seat of faith. This is why prayer is a science of the heart rather than of the mind. St. Thomas tells us that our minds become one with things we can understand. The mind identifies itself with things it sees in the world around us. For those things that are beyond us and that are incomprehensible to us, we can identify with them, becoming one with them, through that other godlike faculty we possess known as our wills. What we cannot understand with our minds because of a truth's incomprehensibility, we can reach up to it with our hearts and embrace it and thus become one with it. Pascal once said that the heart has thoughts that the mind knows nothing of. Love unites and makes itself one with the object loved.

III. Children operate on instinct, and they have an uncanny way of intuiting good and bad people. If a child thinks a person to be good, most likely that person is a good person. If we can stand the test of a child's simplicity, chances are we are in good shape. Charles Dickens wrote of children, "I love these little people: it is no slight thing when they, who are so fresh from God's hand, love us."

IV. God loves simplicity. He doesn't expect us to do such things that will carve out a place for us in history. He desires that we do simple, ordinary things for the motive of pleasing Him; that is, out of sincere love for Him. This transforms our ordinary actions into extraordinary ones in God's eyes. Simple people are devoid of ulterior motives for doing things. Their motive is generally evident, and it is basically one of love, love of God, and love of their brothers and sisters.

V. God is inclined to commune with simple souls and bestow upon them a more enriched prayer life. St. Catherine of Siena asked the Lord, who frequently appeared to her, why He no longer communicated familiarly with men; the Lord responded that men no longer possessed sufficient simplicity. Instead, He said, they appropriate to themselves the lights and gifts which I have given to them. They want Me to listen to them as a disciple (*Dialogues of St. Catherine of Siena*).

1) Our Lord thanked His Father for hiding the mysteries of the kingdom of heaven from the wise and prudent of this world and for revealing them to little ones. When Jesus threw the money changers out of the temple, the children cried out in spontaneous approval and shouted, "Hosanna to the Son of David." The Holy Spirit had to have inspired them to say that, because "Son of David" is a messianic title (Mt. 21:15).

2) When the Pharisees became indignant at this and called Jesus' attention to this, Our Lord answered: "Have you never read 'From the mouths of children and babes in arms you have made sure of praise'?" (Mt.21:16). Here again, God inspires the simple, the humble, and the detached of this world to praise Him.

3) Simplicity gives us an intimacy with God in our prayer lives. It is just as the adage would have it: like things attract one another. Simplicity is truth, and God is its author. Our Lord Jesus Christ had one burning desire: to please His Father in all He did. That is simplicity at its best, a pure, evident, and single motive.

VI. St. Francis of Assisi called simplicity "the sister of wisdom." It is the virtue that strips us of all guile and imparts that freshness that is so evident in children. It frees us of the deceit of sophistication. It is an enemy of deceit and frees us from all guile. It liberates us from ulterior motives and duplicity. The simple-hearted person walks with God.

****

1) That God impart to us this childlike virtue of simplicity.

2) That we be spontaneous in expressing our gratitude for favors or things received.

3) That we try to examine our motives for our actions, and that we strive to be free from all selfish and ulterior motives.

4) That we place more emphasis on doing ordinary things well for the love of God.

5) That we consciously strive to make our motive be to please God in all we say and do.

Wednesday, First Week of Advent: Mt. 15:29-37

I. One thing Jesus never did was turn His back on human need. He would even anticipate the request to alleviate human suffering as we see Him doing in today's Gospel. The people did not ask Him for bread; it was He who saw the situation in which, if they were to start their journey back home, they would be overtaken by hunger.

1) "My heart is moved with pity for the crowd. By now they have been with me for three days and have nothing to eat. I do not wish to send them away hungry lest they collapse on the way." If this is so when Jesus faces physical hunger, how much more will it be so in the case of spiritual hunger?

2) With reason, Jesus would go on to institute the Eucharist, to nourish and sustain the divine life to which a soul is raised through baptism, and to help us to share more intimately in that life on our journey toward eternity.

II. Here Jesus gives the crowd ordinary bread miraculously multiplied; later He would give His Apostles the Bread of Life and through them to all subsequent generations.

1) That ordinary bread was consumed by the people and through the process of digestion became part of their own bodies was common knowledge. The Eucharist, or the Bread of Life, on the other hand, is not absorbed into our bloodstream to build up our physical strength and become part of our physical bodies as natural food does. Jesus Christ, whom we receive in Holy Communion, by His divine power absorbs us into Himself by giving us an ever-growing participation in the very life of the Triune God in which we already participate as sons and daughters of God through baptism.

2) That very relationship of sons and daughters, begun in baptism, continues to grow and intensify or comes to a stop, stultifies, or even ceases to exist because that life of God is driven out of the soul by serious sin. Mortal sin severs the bond or relationship we share with God and makes our bodies and souls uninhabitable for Him.

3) Holy Communion is a powerful sacrament of transformation.

It is the sacrament of divine love that endeavors to unite us with God, or as St. Paul would phrase it, engraft us more and more into God's nature and life (Rom. 11:17).

4) It is for us to give ourselves to Our Lord Jesus Christ and collaborate with the Holy Spirit in this marvelous work of sanctification or transformation of our human souls into the godlike people we are destined to become through the merits of Our Lord Jesus Christ.

III. As the Holy Spirit is the bond of love between the Father and the Son, so too for us, Holy Communion is that bond of love between God and us that seals our relationship with Him as sons and daughters, making us participate more and more in the very life and nature of God Himself.

1) May we always hunger for this Bread of heaven and grow more and more in our relationship with God and in our union with the Spouse of our souls, Our Lord and Savior, Jesus Christ. And even though we do not have the consolation of seeing Jesus present in the Eucharist with our eyes, it is a consolation to Almighty God that we believe in Jesus' presence there precisely because He said He would be really and truly present there.

2) This was the one miracle that the Lord worked before the Apostles at the Last Supper, but He did not let them see Himself in that first Holy Communion during that first Mass. Like the Apostles, Our Lord Jesus Christ demands also of us a deep act of faith and belief in His abiding presence in the Eucharist. As Our Lord said to Thomas, "Blessed are they who have not seen and yet have believed" (Jn. 20:29).

****

1) That our love for God steadily grow through the sacrament of the Eucharist.

2) That our desire to receive Our Lord Jesus Christ in this sacrament be always sincere and earnest.

3) That we prepare the evening before by cultivating a longing to receive Our Lord, Body, Blood, Soul, and Divinity, the following day.

4) That we strive to be ever conscious of whom we receive so we never receive mechanically or out of routine.

5) That we strive to eliminate those obstacles, the sins and faults, which impede our union with Our Lord and God.

6) That our Catholic people come to appreciate more and more the value of this great gift of the Eucharist.

Thursday, First Week of Advent: Mt. 7:24-27

I. Even from a human standpoint, Jesus knew about building houses since He Himself was a carpenter. The winter rains in Palestine could rapidly fill streams with sudden large volumes of water which were capable of eroding the bases of hills and thus causing cave-ins similar to those that happen in California in its rainy season.

1) Houses built on apparently safe hilltops could easily tumble down as the streams erode the base of those hillocks. One would be much wiser to build on rocky ground to be safe.

2) Knowledge of the dangers inherent in a given environment and geography is worthless unless one takes steps to be assured against such dangers. One can easily be lulled into a disbelief of such dangers by the sheer beauty of a building site in the dry season with the scenes it may overlook and go ahead to construct a house on such terrain.

3) So it is with the Gospel: it is not enough to hear its message, we must take it into ourselves and anchor it to the rock of our hearts by making it part of us to the extent that we organize our lives in accord with it.

II. The word of God is a two-edged sword which brings either death or life. There is simply no middle ground. Its sharp edge severs in two those who are either for Christ or against Him. There is no middle ground in Christianity. Our Lord said you are either with Him or against Him. The lukewarm He will vomit from His mouth (Rev. 3:16). From this we get a principle in the spiritual life: there is no standing still; you either advance spiritually or fall back. Going heavenward is like an automobile going uphill; while the motor continues to propel it forward, on it goes. Should the motor stall out, it will naturally be inclined to roll backward.

1) There are many so-called Christians who have all sorts of religious pendants hanging from the rearview mirrors of their cars,

while at the same time they think nothing of engaging in all sorts of vice.

2) For such people, religious articles are nothing more than good-luck charms which quell and appease their superstitions or religious needs in a false way. They are analogous to prostitutes who insist on having religious pictures on their bedroom walls. It really is nothing short of hypocrisy.

III. The Gospel of Our Lord Jesus Christ is God's message to us which, when faithfully carried out, brings us rich rewards both in this life and in eternity.

1) Many hear the message, admire it but, like the seed that fell among thorns, find it too difficult, or they are so caught up with worldly affairs that the Gospel's message is never reduced to practice.

2) The Gospel is not only to be admired when listened to, but it must be taken in to bring about a thorough conversion. When one has become convinced of it, he/she must react to its moving power and mobilize the Gospel's message into deeds. Such was the case in so many lives of great men and women and canonized saints.

3) Such was the case with John Newton, the author of "Amazing Grace." He captained ships plying slaves from Africa to the Americas, when the sheer horror of what he was lending his hand and his skill to got to him through reflecting on the words of the Gospel. He began to feel like a hypocrite; reading the Gospel message was one thing, but putting it into practice was another. He resolved to quit his lucrative position and change his life. He entered the seminary, became an Anglican priest, and used his musical talent to evangelize the ignorant people of the rural English countryside. He would sing the Gospel message to people who could neither read nor write and have them memorize it through songs and hymns. One such hymn he composed was a confession of his past and the story of his conversion. It is called "Amazing Grace." It opens: "Amazing grace! how sweet the sound / That saved a wretch like me! / I once was lost, but now am found, / Was blind, but now I see."

4) We, too, who hear the words of the Gospel should challenge ourselves and ask ourselves, "Am I really putting it into practice, or do I find myself in the rut of indifference?" "Not all those who cry out, 'Lord, Lord,' will enter the kingdom of heaven, but only those

who do the will of my Father." Talk is cheap; deeds bear testimony, the testimony of witness that moves others, especially those who have their houses built on sandy ground.

****

1) That we strive to live the message of Our Lord Jesus Christ in our daily lives.

2) That we always hunger for knowledge of God and for an ever deeper understanding of the Gospel.

3) That the Lord bless us with strong and enlightened convictions about our faith.

4) For priests who preach the word of God, that they live it and encourage others to do so.

5) For an increase in vocations to the priesthood and religious life.

Friday, First Week of Advent: Mt. 9:27-31

I. "I once was . . . blind, but now I see" are the words of the hymn "Amazing Grace." Centuries of Christian testimony and writings have equated faith with light and with sight. Faith is that infused virtue, the instrument, and the means of understanding divine things.

1) St. Paul says that faith comes through hearing, and according to St. John of the Cross, the understanding is the ear of the soul. While understanding is a gift of the Holy Spirit, faith, the infused theological virtue, is the eye of the soul.

2) Dionysius the Areopagite, an early mystical writer of the Church, called faith "a ray of darkness." Perhaps faith can be likened to a little night-light that is left on in a corridor at night to illuminate it with its inconspicuous, muffled light. Perhaps faith can be likened to moonlight, which sheds its subdued light on the objects of night and causes them to cast clear and distinct shadows.

II. St. Augustine said, "Faith is believing what we do not see, and the reward of this faith is to see what we believe."

1) Faith is that supernatural light which enables us to grasp and understand certain truths without seeing them.

2) St. Thomas Aquinas calls faith the dawn of the Beatific Vision. The Bible calls faith that inner light or God's revelation

19

made to our minds and hearts. St. John calls it "the light that illumines and enlightens every man who comes into the world" (Jn. 1:9). St. John of the Cross calls faith "the feet that bear us to God."

3) In his Apostolic Letter on Augustine of Hippo, Pope John Paul II writes, "He [Augustine] also emphasizes that faith is never without reason, because it is reason that shows 'in what one should believe. For faith has its own eyes, by means of which it sees in a certain manner that which it does not yet see is true.' Therefore 'no one believes anything, unless he has first thought that it is to be believed,' because 'to believe is itself nothing other than to think with assent. . . . If faith is not thought through, it is no faith' " (*Origins*, Vol. 16, No. 16).

III. When cataract surgery was first perfected, not so long ago, Marius Von Senden began to collect firsthand accounts from people who had been born blind. They narrated experience of a wonderful excitement over seeing color, light, things, and people. It was like entering into a new world of fantasy (*Weekday Homily Helps*, 1983).

1) Von Senden reported that many of them were frightened and struggled with how to cope with all of the new information — like a baby coming out of the womb. They literally had to learn "to see" to interpret all of this marvelous information.

2) Helen Keller was left blind and deaf in her infancy. When Anne Sullivan introduced her to the world through the alphabet, it was like a gift of faith that enabled her to "see" and understand the world about her without seeing with her physical eyes. Faith is like seeing a new world without being able to see or feel or hear with our physical faculties.

IV. In curing the two blind men of today's Gospel, Christ gave them the joy and happiness of being able to see with their eyes. He gave them more by imparting the gift of faith to the eyes of their souls, so that they could interpret in faith the information the eyes of their souls reported to them of the world about them.

1) Only faith can make us truly see; that is, to be able to understand what we see in this world in relationship to God and eternity. God infuses this understanding into our minds and enables us to judge things and people in a spiritual perspective.

2) Only men and women of faith can penetrate the superficial surfaces of our materialistic world. Faith affords us the light to

penetrate the covering of human pride and sensuality. Only faith can tell us the true worth of the things of this world.

3) Only faith can give us the light to see Jesus in the outcasts of society: the poor, and the marginated of this world. Would that we all could say, "I . . . was blind and now I see."

****

1) Faith is a gift that only God can give. No one can earn it and no university can impart it; let us frequently ask God for an increase in faith.

2) That all those who have lost the faith may recover it through the mercy of God.

3) For all of those who are experiencing doubts in their faith or who are drifting, especially members of our own families, that the Lord increase their faith.

4) That the young come to love the word of God and find light and strength from the Bible.

5) That the Lord bestow upon all of us the gift of prayer, and that through this gift we may be in constant communication with God during the day, making our work itself a prayer.

6) That all of us persevere in our faith until death, and that through the intercession of the Blessed Virgin Mary we be graced with the sacraments before leaving this world.

Saturday, First Week of Advent: Mt. 9:35-10:I, 6-8

I. As paradoxical as it may seem, God will harvest souls without human laborers. He wills to work through us weak human instruments. It fits so well into the doctrine and overall picture of the Mystical Body of Christ. Jesus is Head of that Body, and we are the members. Just as the Head needs the body to operate, so too do the members need that Head for direction and light.

1) "The harvest is great, but the laborers are scarce." The Lord wills the salvation of all men and women, but He will not harvest those souls without the aid of generous laborers. He calls many of us to go forth into the field to bring in that harvest, but alas, so many refuse to go.

2) It is so like the parable of the two sons who were asked by their father to go into the vineyard to work. The first said "no," but

21

later repented and went; the second said "yes," but didn't go. It is similar to the workers of the harvest: the response is not enthusiastic.

3) Pope Leo the Great observed in his day (fifth century) that there was no shortage of priests; rather the ones ordained were not doing the work they were called to do (Sermon 92, Office of Readings).

II. Today the Church is suffering from a serious shortage of priests. In 1980, there were 58,000 American priests. That number declined by 571 over the previous decade of the '70s, and the average age is climbing significantly.

1) Total seminary enrollment fell from 45,700 to 13,200 between 1967 and 1980 (Francis Kelly Scheets, O.S.C., "Will There BE Seminarians in 1990? A Plan of Action for the 1980s"). In 1940, the laity-clergy relationship was one to 640: in 1985 it was one to 1,100.

2) In France, there are 1,500 parishes that celebrate Sunday liturgies without a priest. In some dioceses of Germany and the Netherlands as many as 40 percent of the parishes lack a priest. In the Third World mission countries, about half of all parishes and missions stations are without a priest (*Pastoral Life*, Dec., 1981).

3) Pope John Paul II said, "The problem of priestly vocations is the fundamental problem of the Church. It is the verification of the spiritual vitality and the condition of its mission and development."

4) The majority of diocesan priests will be in the 46-to-75-year-old bracket throughout the decade of the '90s. Parents are not encouraging their children to aspire to the priesthood. In 1979, George Gallup made a survey of the attitude of Catholic parents toward desiring to see a son or daughter become a priest or religious. Fifty-four percent said that they did not want to see their son or daughter become a priest or enter the religious life. Only 46 percent said that they would like to see their son or daughter enter the priesthood or religious life. What an indictment of the state of faith in Catholic people of our times!

5) No doubt the great social upheavals of our time have produced unrest and unwillingness among the young to make lifelong commitments. This is evident also in marriages today.

III. Christianity is nearly 2,000 years old. When Jesus ascended to heaven from the Mount of Olives, He commanded His Apostles to go out into the whole world to preach the Good News. This command is given to all of us; we all must bear the message of the Gospel. After 2,000 years, a little better than one in five persons is Christian. One of the reasons the Gospel hasn't reached so many is that there aren't enough laborers in the field to bring in the harvest.

IV. Whatever the objections and criticisms, the priesthood still remains a sublime calling. The priest is the necessary vehicle between God and men. Only he can offer the holy Sacrifice of the Mass, forgive sins, and anoint the sick. His ministry is most intimately connected with the salvation of souls. The priesthood will always be a *sine qua non*, an absolutely indispensable sacrament, which can only be conferred on the legitimately called and voluntarily responsive young men, and of which Our Lord Jesus Christ will always be the eternal model — the generous servant of the servants of the poor.

****

1) Our Lord gave us the means to obtain an increase of vocations: "Pray the Lord of the harvest that he send laborers into the harvest." That we all commit ourselves to pray hard for good and generous vocations.

2) That parents realize what a unique privilege it is to have a son as priest, who can always remember them at the altar of God, and that they encourage their sons who express such a desire.

3) That parents pray that the Lord touch one of their sons or daughters with a vocation to follow Him in the priesthood or religious life.

4) That all those who feel the Lord calling them to the priesthood or to the religious life may respond to this sublime calling.

5) That priests and religious collaborate with those generous graces that the Lord gives them so that they may give inspiration to others through their own zealous and happy lives.

Monday, Second Week of Advent: Lk. 5:17-26

I. The reading from Isaiah foretells the messianic age. In so many words Isaiah is saying that God's activity in bringing Israel from slavery to freedom at the time of their exodus from Babylon was not an isolated event. Just as the Lord was present at Israel's exodus from Egypt, so too was He present at their delivery from the

Babylonians. In short, God is present at every deliverance, be it of a nation, a group, or an individual.

II. Isaiah speaks here of a new exodus in tremendous outbursts of joy and confidence; it is an exodus from sin and misery. "The blind will see, the deaf will hear" (Is. 35:5). Isaiah sees the coming of Christ as a new and definitive exodus. He foresees freedom from the servitude to sin and to the devil.

1) A new kingdom will appear: the presence of God among men, the kingdom of God on earth.

2) Those renewed by the presence of God will experience freedom and a change in the way they perceive reality.

III. In today's Gospel, we see the fulfillment of Isaiah's prophecy: the paralytic is released from the bonds of his physical affliction; more still, he is freed from the bondage of his sins. What joy entered his heart!

IV. The paralytic had faith. Certainly his stretcher-bearers did. The critical scribes and Pharisees did not. They prejudiced themselves against anything Jesus might say or do that would move them into a position of accepting Him as the Messiah promised by the prophet Isaiah.

1) Their hearts were simply closed, and what their eyes and ears reported to them, what they were witnessing, would go for naught. This was not the case, however, with the paralytic nor with the humble faith-filled stretcher-bearers. Their confidence and faith in Jesus was so strong that they removed part of the roof covering in order to get Jesus' attention.

2) Jesus' response to such faith is immediate, as it always is, and He reaches out to heal the paralytic, clearly fulfilling the messianic description of Isaiah that the lame would walk. To reveal His messiahship, Jesus first forgives the sins of the paralytic, knowing that this would make the scribes and Pharisees indignant. To reinforce His claim that "the Son of Man has the power to forgive sins," He gives physical healing to the paralytic.

V. The stretcher-bearers in this narrative should not be overlooked here. Their message is loud and clear. They helped the paralytic get to the presence of Jesus. As the paralytic needed their help to bring him to Jesus, God uses other people to bring people in need to Him for spiritual and physical healing.

1) God always works through other human beings in the process of the sanctification and salvation of souls. We are all members of His Mystical Body, and we are our brothers' and sisters' keepers.

2) When Saul of Tarsus was struck down from his horse, blinded, the Lord did not heal him directly. Rather He told Ananias to go to a street named Straight to where Saul (the future St. Paul) was staying and place hands upon him. Ananias did so and Saul received his sight. He was baptized and received the Holy Spirit (Acts 9:10-18).

3) People are the instruments for bringing other people to God. How many people were brought back to the faith because of another person. How many parents brought back their wayward children to the practice of their faith through their tears and prayers. As St. Ambrose said of St. Monica, it is impossible that the child of such tears should perish (he was referring to Augustine). You and I can unwittingly be those stretcher-bearers with a lively faith and zeal for souls who may be God's instruments in bringing souls back to Christ.

****

1) That the Lord fill us with a lively zeal for souls.

2) That we always be disposed to be God's stretcher-bearers in bringing people back to Him.

3) That parents realize the great influence they have on their children and never give up on them.

4) That our faith continue to grow in intensity.

5) That we persevere in our prayer and always be mindful to express our gratitude to Almighty God for His immense goodness shown to us.

6) For all the sick of the parish, that they bear their illnesses with patience and as an offering for the conversion of sinners, and that the Lord restore them to health.

Tuesday, Second Week of Advent: Mt. 18:12-14

I. The salvation of souls is God's supreme law, and this parable of the lost sheep is such a graphic picture of God's burning love for His creatures.

II. The parable struck home with a very meaningful message to the people of Palestine, for so many people had sheep and depended on them for their livelihood. To lose even one sheep was to sustain a heavy loss for poor families. Every sacrifice would be made to find the ones that had strayed off from the flock. It was not an uncommon scene to see a shepherd returning with a young stray sheep about his neck. We can imagine the enthusiastic joy in one's family and among one's neighbors upon seeing the shepherd returning with a lost sheep.

III. The life of a shepherd was a precarious one, since pasture was scarce, especially fresh, green pasture, and the sheep had a tendency to wander off in search of it.

1) Sheep are capable of wandering down steep ravines or gullies or of getting themselves into situations from which it would be impossible to extricate themselves. In such helpless situations they would fall easy prey to wolves. A good shepherd would have to risk his life to retrieve sheep which had gotten themselves into precarious situations.

2) A good shepherd might have to go down dangerous ravines, climb steep precipices, go out onto a dangerous rocky ledge, or risk confrontation with vicious mountain wolves traveling in packs, all in an effort to save a stray sheep and return it to safety in its fold.

IV. William Butler Yeats wrote, "The love of God is infinite for every human being, because every human soul is unique; no other can satisfy the same need in God than that particular soul."

1) God's love is universal, yet at the same time it is particular. There is a soft spot in God's Heart for each and every one of us, and He will not be satisfied until all of His sons and daughters are safely home in paradise.

2) With reason could St. Augustine say: "Our hearts were made for Thee, O Lord, and they will not rest until they rest in Thee."

V. God hungers for our love. To St. Margaret Mary Our Lord said: "Behold the Heart that has loved men so much and is so little loved in return." God thirsts for our love so ardently that He sent His only begotten Son, to redeem us and make it possible for us to be with Him forever.

1) Once a person's love has been purified and cultivated, says St. John of the Cross, "A little of this love is more precious in the sight of God and of greater profit to the Church, even though the person

engaged in it seems to be doing nothing, than all exterior works together" (*Spiritual Canticle*, XXIX, 2).

2) St. Teresa of Jesus (Ávila) wrote: "I believe, Lord, that if it were possible for me to hide myself from You, as You hide from me, Your love for me would not tolerate my hiding from You."

VI. God pursues us down the corridors of time. One of the best religious poems of the English language is Francis Thompson's "Hound of Heaven." The poet describes his running away from God. He compares God to a dog chasing after his soul. Thompson had contracted an opium habit that wrecked him and reduced him to begging in the slums of England. However much he would try to turn away, God was hounding him until the poet surrendered to His pursuing love and returned to the flock and soul-saving pasture.

VII. From creation and redemption we have a natural and supernatural resemblance to God. This divine resemblance best expresses God's desire to unite souls to Himself, to transform us more and more into Him. He who created this resemblance wills to bring it to completion, but He will not do it without our response in a similar return of love.

****

1) That we express our gratitude to Almighty God in sending the Good Shepherd into the world in the person of Our Lord, Jesus Christ.

2) That we frequently and sincerely express our love for God in our hearts and souls.

3) That the Holy spirit enkindle within us the fire of His love.

4) That we too help the Lord search out and bring back souls that have strayed away.

5) That people who are careless or indifferent about their faith may come to realize how foolish their position is.

6) That none of us or members of our families be ever separated from God's favor, nor that His passion and death for us be in vain.

Wednesday, Second Week of Advent: Mt. 11:28-30

I. Jesus is the map of eternal life; He sums this up in today's Gospel by telling us that He is the way, the truth, and the life. Without Jesus Christ, there would be no knowing the truth, no road or way, and certainly no possibility of attaining to eternal life, because we would not have the wherewithal to attain it.

II. The consequence of all this is obedience to the way He has shown us. Both truth and obedience have the power of freeing us. Disobedience blinds one to pride, which is nothing but a product of self-love and deceit. Furthermore, disobedience engenders ignorance. Disobedience and ignorance do nothing but shackle and enslave us.

1) St. John writes,"You shall know the truth and the truth shall make you free" (Jn. 8:32). Truth is not always easy to face or to carry out, because its enemies are formidable: they are the devil, our own selfish fallen nature with its unruly passions, and the lure and fallacious enticements of the world in which we live, with all its flashy, gaudy, ephemeral deceit.

2) However difficult a given truth may be to carry out in our daily lives, if we do it for someone we love, it becomes a light burden. Love has that quality of making the difficult easy and the burdensome light. The famous motto of Father Flanagan's Boys Town sums this truth up well: an older boy carrying a younger boy on his back responds to Father Flanagan, "He ain't heavy, Father, he's my brother."

III. In fulfilling the commandments of God and the duties inherent in our state in life, let us always remember that He bears that yoke with us; we don't go it alone. For this reason Christ calls His way a sweet yoke and a light burden. Where Christ Jesus is, there is sweetness; where Christ is, there is no burden.

1) This is true for the sacrament of marriage. It is not only a commitment between a man and a woman; it is a three-way pact. Through the conferral of this sacrament on each other, the husband and wife draw Jesus Christ into the covenant with them. He then is committed to shoulder the burdens of married life with them. The more Christ-centered that marriage is, the sweeter its yoke and the lighter its burdens become, for the Lover par excellence sweetens the yoke.

2) The same thing can be said for the yoke of holy orders. The priest doesn't shoulder the burdens inherent in the priestly work alone; Jesus Christ, the eternal High Priest, will gladly lighten that burden. The closer a priest strives to do his work with Jesus Christ,

the sweeter and more attractive it becomes. Like the sacrament of matrimony, it becomes the source of happiness to him.

3) When a horse and a mule are yoked together, the mule will allow the horse to do all the work. When Our Lord Jesus Christ embraces the yoke of His way with us, a perfect team is made, for what we lack He will supply; what we cannot do, He will do to bring us along that way to a perfect union with our heavenly Father.

IV. The yoke of the Lord is summed up in one saying: to love the Lord our God with our whole hearts, minds, and souls and our brothers and sisters as ourselves.

1) The happiest people in this world are those who make great sacrifices and give of themselves in the service of others. This has been consistently evident in the lives of the saints. In our own times, Mother Teresa has given a sparkling example of such service, her face radiating inner joy, peace, and happiness. The Lord will not be outdone in generosity; He rewards generous, sacrificial people with rich spiritual gifts. When we serve others, we serve the Lord, and He is not slow to repay.

2) Loving difficult people can be very demanding, but it becomes light when we undertake to serve them for the Lord, who is their Creator also.

3) Experience shows us that when we sacrifice our time or go out of our way to do something for a needy person, a handicapped person, a shut-in, an elderly or ill person, there is a built-in instant reward of "feeling good" about having done it. This is God's way of saying, "Thank you; I am pleased."

****

1) To look frequently upon the crucifix in loving gratitude for what Our Lord has done for us.

2) When we feel the urge to complain, let us reflect that when we bear difficult things, it is a pleasing and meritorious penance.

3) That we be generous in responding to the needs of others.

4) That we strive to lighten the burdens of others, especially of fellow workers, and be a source of cheerfulness to those with whom we live and work.

5) That we remember that a thoughtful visit does much to make another feel better.

6) For peace in the world, an end to the arms race, and an end to terrorism.

Thursday, Second Week of Advent: Mt. 11:11-15

I. Jesus paid no higher tribute to any other human being than He did to John the Baptist. He was a stalwart, loyal servant of God who was fearlessly committed to his sublime vocation.

1) He told the truth as God gave the light and the strength to do so. It meant confronting the scribes and Pharisees and calling them to task for their hypocrisy and deceit.

2) He even confronted King Herod for his incestuous relationship. This eventually brought down Herod's wrath upon him and hastened John's martyrdom.

II. "The kingdom of heaven suffers violence," says Our Lord Jesus Christ, "and the violent take it by force" (Mt. 11:12). John the Baptist paid the price of his loyalty to God by laying down his life. He met the violence of persecution with the violence of his virtue of loyalty and fidelity even in the face of death.

1) St. Thomas More also paid for his loyalty to his faith, and as much as he loved life, his family, and his work, he would not compromise his virtue even to the pressures put upon him by King Henry VIII, or by his friends and family. He would lay down his life rather than water down his convictions or his loyalty to God.

2) Mother Elizabeth Ann Seton was cut off from her inheritance because she converted to Catholicism, and in spite of the crisis of the death of her husband and the loss of his business, she would not compromise her loyalty to her Catholic faith in order to receive financial help from her relatives. She was to go on to take heaven by storm, by the violence of her fidelity and persistent loyalty to her faith.

III. Our Lord Jesus Christ is telling us in so many words that no one gets a free ride into the kingdom of heaven. No Christian just "drifts in." There is no easy way. For all good things we must pay a heavy price. Heaven is no exception. Jesus counsels the narrow way of the cross: "Enter by the narrow gate; for the gate is wide and the way is easy that leads to destruction, and those who enter by it are many" (Mt. 7:13).

1) Loyalty to Christ will cost us, and there can be no middle way

of compromise. We will be either with Him or against Him. The soft, sensual, comfort-seeking philosophy of the world will never win the rewards of heaven.

2) We are to be light and salt to the world and stalwart witnesses to the Gospel message. We must never be afraid to stand up and be counted, and in doing so we will not be free of persecution. In Our Lord's own words, the Son of Man came to bring "not peace but a sword, to set father against son, mother against daughter, and mother-in-law against daughter-in-law, and a man's foes will be those of his own household" (Mt. 10:34-36).

3) Loyalty to our faith will at times demand the brute violence in the courage of steadfast virtue. It is such violence that takes heaven by storm. Sometimes it may involve the violence of death. The Boxer Rebellion was a movement in China that attempted to drive out foreigners and stamp out Christianity. When its revolutionaries captured a mission school in 1900, they blocked all the gates but one. On the ground in front of that gate they laid a cross. Anyone who would trample upon that cross would go free; anyone who endeavored to walk around it would be shot to death. The first seven students trampled on the cross and went free. The eighth, a teenage girl, knelt before the cross, then walked respectfully around it. She was killed immediately. The rest of the students, 100 in all, followed that gallant girl's example and were killed. Over 30,000 Chinese chose death rather than deny Our Lord Jesus Christ. What steadfast loyalty! (A. Tonne, *Five-Minute Homilies on the Gospels, A, B, C*).

IV. St. John's last book of the New Testament, the Book of Revelation, is a plea for loyalty and patient, persevering faith: "To the angel of the church at Smyrna, write, '. . . I know your tribulation and your poverty. . . . Do not fear what you are about to suffer. Behold the devil is about to throw some of you into prison, that you may be tested. . . . Be faithful to death, and I will give you the crown of life' " (Rev. 2:8-10).

1) "To the angel of the church at Philadelphia write: '. . . Because you have kept my words with perseverance, I for my part will protect you in the hour of your trial. . . . I will come soon. Remain faithful; do not let anyone snatch your crown away!" (Rev. 3:10-12).

2) In all probability we will not be asked to put our lives on the

line in regard to our faith, but if we put the Gospel into practice in our daily lives, we will be the butt of criticism, scorn, and other types of persecution.

****

1) That the Lord give us the grace to remain faithful and courageous witnesses of His Gospel.

2) That we be psychologically prepared for criticism, abuse, and persecution as we strive to live faithfully the Lord's message.

3) That we be mindful to offer up the merit gained from bearing the trials of persecution at times for the holy souls in purgatory.

4) That the criminal violence that abounds in the world today come to an end, especially the violence of terrorism.

5) That the violence of the whole drug-trafficking scene may cease, and that the power of drugs over our young be broken.

6) For peace in the world, an end to the arms race, and the conversion of the Soviet Union.

Friday, Second Week of Advent: Mt. 11:16-19

I. Children are often contrary and cantankerous; no matter what is said or done, often it is difficult to please them. It is a facet of the perversity of our fallen nature damaged by Original Sin. When children want their own way, they will not accept substitute measures.

II. We often hear of people being so set in their ways that anything new or unaccustomed to them is just out of the question. Jesus' lifestyle should have been attractive to many devout Jews, because they were tired of rigorous and detailed obligations from the scribes and Pharisees.

1) In spite of the Pharisees boasting of their strict observance of the law, they were doing their own thing behind the scenes. John the Baptist called them hypocrites for this, even calling them a "brood of vipers."

2) Jesus also criticized them for their perversity, likening them to cantankerous children who want everything their way. They wanted a Messiah to suit their tastes. They rejected John the Baptist for being too rigorous; they now reject Jesus because He is too liberal.

III. The plain fact is that some people just do not want to listen to the truth, or if they must listen to it, they have an uncanny knack of filtering it through a selective process, accepting what they like and refusing to take in what they dislike. They turn their hearing on or off depending on what is agreeable and suitable to them.

1) How true this is in the lives of every one of us: when we are confronted with a difficult message we readily find excuses not to listen or accept it.

2) Bitter pills, however beneficial they might be, are extremely distasteful to children. The Gospel calls for a change of heart, a change in lifestyle. Like St. Augustine before his conversion, we too say, "Lord, not yet; I'm not ready."

IV. We see much of this cantankerousness in people today who continue to criticize the Church since Vatican II.

1) Some want a return to the past. Others feel we haven't moved or advanced far enough. Some say that the Church has become too liberal and has made too many concessions; others hold she hasn't made enough concessions and remains too conservative.

2) The Church is moving toward perfection and must undergo growing pains in the process. Growth always involves change in adjusting ourselves to the unfamiliar. The Church is you and me tied in with Jesus Christ to form what is called the Mystical Body of Christ, of which He is the Head and we are the members. Since we make up part of the whole, it is imperfect and must move toward perfection. Vatican II calls the Church "the seed and beginning" of the kingdom Jesus proclaimed, which yearns and strives for its perfection and consummation (*Dogmatic Constitution on the Church*, No. 5).

3) If we may paraphrase a remark by Lincoln, "You can't please all of the people all of the time." If people are determined not to make a response to any overture, they will not make it no matter how strongly they are urged to do so.

V. Jesus concludes: "Wisdom is shown to be right by her deeds"; that is, by her works: the lives and works of John the Baptist and Jesus. The ultimate verdict on John the Baptist and Jesus will lie not with the criticism of the scribes, the Pharisees, or with criticism of perverse, cantankerous people, but with the positive fruit of their message and their works. History bears them out.

1) Jesus is calling for its openness and sincerity in the search for

truth, even if this should involve a certain amount of risk. The risk involved is the risk of faith.

2) We must not allow our prejudices to color our reception for the message of the Gospel; nor must we permit it to be interpreted by a secular and sensual world, but by the magisterium of the Church as our safe criterion and guide.

3) We must learn to sift things out in prayer and take to heart and act on what we recognize as true and beneficial. This is Christian maturity.

****

1) That we always have a deep love of truth no matter what it may cost us in applying it to our lives.

2) That we desire to know ourselves and our own shortcomings so as to strive to eliminate them and grow.

3) That God bless us with a deep humility in our search for truth, and that we always have a reverence and respect for the teaching authority of the Church as it is expressed through its magisterium.

4) That we always reflect in meditative prayer on the Gospel message and beg God for the wisdom and prudence to apply it to ourselves.

5) That the Lord bless us with that instinct to decipher the deceit of the devil, who constantly strives to pervert the Gospel message by sowing the seeds of confusion.

6) The doctrine of Our Lord Jesus Christ is the doctrine of the narrow way; that we never water down the teaching of the Gospel in order to accommodate ourselves to the philosophy of the world.

7) That God bless us with a true and sincere contrition for our sins.

Saturday, Second Week of Advent: Mt. 17:10-13

I. The lives of Elijah, John the Baptist, and Jesus follow the same tragic pattern. The three were neither recognized nor accepted for who and what they were.

1) Elijah was a staunch defender of traditional Israelite morality, and he was in constant fear of his life at the hands of King Ahab and Queen Jezebel of Israel. The king and queen viewed Elijah as a troublesome critic of their policies and behavior.

2) John the Baptist had to suffer and eventually would die because King Herod and his cohorts feared the effects of John's ministry and preaching.

3) Finally, Jesus Himself was rejected by the elders and leaders of the Jewish community because they viewed Him as a threat to their position of authority.

II. The Jewish people believed that Elijah would indeed return to prepare the people for the coming of the Messiah. This belief was voiced in the prophecy of Malachi: "Behold, I will send you Elijah, the prophet, before the great and terrible day of the Lord comes" (Mal. 3:23). When the Archangel Gabriel foretold the birth of John the Baptist to Zechariah, he said that John would "go before him [the Messiah] in the spirit and the power of Elijah, to turn the hearts of fathers to their children and the rebellious to the wisdom of the just, and to prepare for the Lord a people well-disposed" (Lk. 1:17).

1) Jesus tells the people, "I assure you that Elijah has already come, but they did not recognize him, and did as they pleased with him" (Mt. 16:12). Jesus was in reality speaking of John the Baptist, for John embodied the spirit of Elijah.

2) As so many prophets, including Elijah, were victims of abuse and persecution, so it was with John the Baptist, and so it would be with the Messiah, Jesus Christ, the Son of God made man.

3) In spite of His rejection, Jesus had come to establish God's kingdom on earth and to restore all things under the dominion of His kingship.

4) It is in the mystery of apparent contradiction, rejection, suffering, and persecution that the message of God still comes through loud and clear. It is the power of God's grace that moves the divine plan forward to establish His kingdom on earth, to facilitate the salvation of souls, and this in spite of whatever obstacles demons or humans might bring forth to block it.

III. This mystery of suffering, persecution, and rejection will invariably be tied up with the propagation of the Gospel throughout the world.

1) Each and every Christian during the course of his/her life, will feel these contradictions, persecutions, and rejections being directed at him/her, if he/she is really bearing witness to the Gospel.

2) This will always be so while evil exists in this world and the

forces of hate work to block the salvific message of Our Lord Jesus Christ. The death of so many martyrs bears testimony to this. Our Lord promised His disciples a hundredfold reward in this life for following Him in total dedication — and persecution besides, and in the age to come life everlasting (Mk. 10:28-30).

3) We must be prepared to be victims of this in one form or another, with greater or lesser intensity, at various times in our lives, but this should not surprise us, "for what they have done to the Master they will do to you." The Lord assures us that if we persevere we will receive the crown of life. The suffering caused by bloody or unbloody persecutions wins the graces to extend God's kingdom on earth. In the early Church it was the blood of martyrs that was the seed of faith and freedom for Christianity in the Roman Empire.

IV. St. Paul in his Second Letter to Timothy wrote, "This is the Gospel I preach; in preaching it I suffer as a criminal, even to the point of being thrown into chains — but there is no chaining the word of God! Therefore I bear with all of this for the sake of those whom God has chosen, in order that they may obtain the salvation to be found in Christ Jesus and with it eternal glory" (2 Tim. 2:8-10).

1) We all are called upon to make sacrifices for our brothers and sisters, especially the sacrifice involved in good example. In a world inundated by media propagating a humanism that is at variance with the Gospel, weak Christians are afraid to do the good they feel they want to, because they feel that they will stand out as being different and will be criticized for it.

2) Pope Paul VI said, "Modern man listens more willingly to witnesses than to teachers, and if he does listen to teachers it is because they are witnesses."

****

1) That the Lord increase our faith.

2) That He give us strength to endure abuse, criticism, persecution, and rejection in bearing witness to His Gospel.

3) Our Lord Jesus Christ will always be a sign of contradiction, as the prophet Simeon foretold during the presentation of the infant Jesus in the Temple. May hardened sinners see in Him a sign of compassion and mercy, so that they may return to their faith.

4) For all those who are weak in their faith and lack discipline in

their own moral lives, that during the period of Advent they may come to realize their plight, be touched by the grace of repentance, and place the values of eternity over those of time.

5) That through the intercession of St. John the Baptist the Holy Spirit fill us with fortitude in witnessing to the Gospel in our daily lives.

6) That we recognize the value of sustaining criticism, persecution, and rejection as a valuable penance and excellent means of winning graces for ourselves and others.

Monday, Third Week of Advent: Mt. 21:23-27

I. Jesus acted boldly for the sake of teaching the Gospel. This often left the chief priests and elders beside themselves and seething with anger. Such things as overturning the tables of the money changers and driving out the cattle from the temple precincts was an affront to their authority. His teaching and preaching in the Temple left the crowds in awe and diminished the prestige of the elders, chief priests, scribes, and Pharisees. Jesus' triumphant entry into Jerusalem was the tip of the iceberg — the straw that broke the camel's back. They had to do something to stop Him before the crowds would make Him a king.

1) The chief priests decided to challenge Him: "By what authority do you do these things?" Jesus responds by challenging them: "Was John's baptism from heaven or from men?"

2) Jesus confronts them with the sign of the times. John is a herald, a holy man, and a prophet. Why are they not accepting him? Now Jesus will give them the same treatment they were giving John by remaining silent about him. He will not answer their question because they are not truthful.

II. As members of the Sanhedrin, they were the official teachers of the Jewish community. These chief priests and elders were the legitimately qualified authority to determine true from false prophets. Evidence was overwhelming with John the Baptist, but they would not commit themselves to a public recognition of John, since John was condemning their hypocrisy.

1) Jesus is evidently challenging the chief priests and elders to speak the truth since it was their duty to do so. If they admitted that the ministry of John was from God, they would have to admit Jesus

as Messiah, because John preached this and pointed Jesus out as the One who was to come into the world to save it. This was all the more reason they would not endorse John.

2) If they should deny that John's ministry was from God, they would incur the wrath of the people, for they all accepted John as a prophet and a man of truth. They opt for the easy way out by remaining silent. This amounts to cowardice. Silence admits guilt.

III. How easy it is to remain silent on vital issues, but how wrong this is, especially when one holds a position of authority or is otherwise obligated to speak!

1) What prompts silence so often is fear, but to submit to such fear is cowardice.

2) Politicians are often guilty of this by supporting not what they honestly believe in but what will win them the most votes. Principles go down the drain, or they are compromised by such expressions as, "I am personally opposed to abortion, but I won't impose my views on others." This is nothing more than pure expediency and cowardice.

IV. We too find ourselves in situations where we ask ourselves what is the expedient thing to say or the safer way to act, not what is the right thing to say or do.

1) If a person knows the truth and is under the obligation to reveal it when legitimate authority asks pertinent questions or the common good demands that he/she profess it, cowardice and expediency must be suppressed.

2) To resort to the "I don't know" of the chief priests and elders is nothing more than lying. Truth demands courage, the courage of our convictions, and this is expected of all of us. Truth must be lived. To live it is really to bear witness to the Gospel as Our Lord Jesus Christ exhorts us to. To practice the silence of the chief priests, elders, scribes, or the expediency and compromise of politicians is a sellout of the Gospel and is unworthy of the dignity of one's Christianity.

3) St. Bernard wrote, "When the truth shines out in a soul, and the soul sees itself in the truth, there is nothing brighter than that light or more impressive than that testimony. . . . Shining out like rays upon the body, it makes it a mirror of itself so that its beauty

appears in a man's every action, his speech, his looks, his movements, and his smile" (cited in *Pastoral Life*).

****

1) That we strive to be honest in all our undertakings and dealings with others.

2) That we be especially honest and open in the sacrament of penance and reconciliation.

3) That we do make our feelings and opinions on important issues known to our senators and congressmen.

4) That the Lord give us fortitude and courage to reveal the truth when it is our duty to do so.

5) That salespersons and all business people not resort to lying, in the form of cheating, in order to make a sale.

6) That our American people take a sense of pride in their work, and that honesty reign between employers and employees.

7) That those in legislative or executive positions not submit to the deceit of taking bribes.

Tuesday, Third Week of Advent: Mt. 21:28-32

I. The old adage "Actions speak louder than words" is the message of today's Gospel.

II. When the Pharisees and Sadducees saw so many people going out to John the Baptist to be baptized, they decided to approach him also about receiving this baptism of repentance. John called them a "brood of vipers," because they were approaching him out of hypocrisy and vanity, for they knew that the people would like that and they would be less likely to lose prestige or acceptance among the people.

1) John tells them to give evidence of their sincerity by deeds. Their positions of authority demanded this of them, for they set themselves up as the interpreters of the law and therefore its exemplars.

2) They were largely hypocrites and patterned their lives on external observances while their hearts were full of rapaciousness and deceit. They approached John as an external gesture; that is, to look good before the masses.

III. The parable of the two sons is directed at both the Pharisees on the one hand and the rejects of society on the other hand.

1) The Pharisees are represented by the first son, who said "yes" to his father's request that he go out into the vineyard to work, but even though his response was immediate, with all the ceremony that might adorn his agreement, in effect, his "yes" terminated in a very real "no."

2) The publicans, harlots, and rabble of society are represented by the second son, whose initial "no" is portrayed by their open lives of sin and recklessness, but they are struck with sincere repentance and have a change of mind and heart. Their initial "no" terminates in a "yes."

IV. Jesus is teaching that sinners who truly repent are closer to salvation than those who consider themselves righteous.

1) Sinners who have ignored God's will and led profligate lives, and who are later touched by the grace of repentance, are like the second son who initially said "no" to his father and later repented.

2) Other people who have the trappings of religion, and who give off all the appearances of a devout "yes" to God's will, actually say "no" in their hearts to His will, and go off to do their own thing away from the eyes of those who know them. These are the hypocrites, like the first son who says "yes" but means "no."

V. Words and promises can never take the place of deeds. Our Lord gives the criterion for true evaluation: "By their fruits you shall know them" (Mt. 7:16).

1) The first son, who graciously said "yes" but did not go into his father's vineyard, had all the outward marks of courtesy but was a phony. This does not mean to belittle those who are courteous. Indeed our "yes" should be gracious as well as earnest and sincere.

2) The second son certainly does not receive an A-plus. He took much of the good out of his final act of obedience.

3) A lack of gracious willingness can well spoil the good we endeavor to do. It turns off people for whom we do a good turn. It makes them feel burdened for having imposed upon us. They will hardly seek us out a second time.

VI. All of this does not mean that we are not going to experience feelings of rebellion surging up within us from the instincts of our fallen nature, especially when we are confronted with something difficult. There is so much more merit to the difficult "yes," which is naturally hard to make with graciousness and ease. Even Our Lord Jesus Christ found it difficult to say yes to the Cross and even asked His Father to allow Him to forgo it. Many things in life are going to be hard. It is then that we must have recourse to prayer to obtain the grace to make an eager "yes" response to something that is our duty to do.

****

1) That we be sincere in all our commitments and undertakings.

2) That we strive to do things and fulfill our obligations cheerfully and graciously.

3) When we foresee that we are going to be confronted with something difficult to do, that we anticipate it with prayer and seek ways to make its undertaking as smooth as possible.

4) That the Lord give us patience in all our trials.

5) That the Lord give us cheerful dispositions.

6) For all statesmen who are negotiating for world peace, that they be filled with tact and patience.

Wednesday, Third Week of Advent: Lk. 7:18-23

I. Judaism had always held that the coming of the Lord would take place with signs of great power and would coincide with a terrible judgment of the nations (Is. 40:10, 51:9). John the Baptist predicts the era of the Lord as a period of fire and destruction (Mt. 3:11-12) (Maertens-Frisque, *Guide for the Christian Assembly*).

II. When Jesus answers the disciples of John who came to inquire if He really was the Christ, He cites the messianic prophecy of Isaiah and concludes with the words "And blessed is he who is not scandalized in me." Jesus is obviously alluding here to their expectancy of fire and destruction and great show of power. Contrary to their expectations, Jesus goes about with meekness and humility. This show of power and destruction and judgment of nations will be reserved for His second coming at the end of the world.

III. The meek and gentle nature of Jesus tries the faith of John the Baptist and his disciples. John wanted to assure his disciples of Jesus' messiahship by having them confront Jesus directly. Jesus allays their doubts by showing how He does indeed fulfill the prophecy of Isaiah: "The blind see, the deaf hear, the lame walk [Is. 35:5-6], and the poor have the good news preached to them" (Lk. 7:22-24).

1) Jesus distinguishes between His coming in mildness, gentleness, compassion, and mercy and His final coming in judgment, when indeed He will manifest the power and majesty of God.

2) Jesus' manifestation of a gentle compassionate Savior scandalizes those who expected One who would come showing the avenging power of God. For those harboring such ideas about the Messiah, Jesus more than proves His messiahship by His abundant miracles, especially those miracles of spiritual and physical healing. For such signs would, according to Isaiah, accompany the Messiah.

IV. Even the great John the Baptist was left to discover that faith is not a once-and-for-all decision. He had pointed out Jesus as the Messiah in the Jordan, and that was final. As with all of us, his faith was also challenged. Jesus was not measuring up to the kind of Messiah he expected, and he was having second thoughts about Jesus. John had to renew his own faith in Him.

1) So it is in the lives of all of us: our faith is going to be tried. Doubts will arise, and we too will have to renew our convictions about our faith. This is necessary for growth.

2) There will be times when we will feel that God has abandoned us. None of our prayers are being heard. Things are not turning out as expected. After being faithful for so long, instead of being rewarded, we seem to be afflicted with a series of awful setbacks. A son or daughter is not turning out the way you hoped, and this after trying so hard to rear him/her. A husband or wife has walked out after so many years. You have been passed over at work for advancement by a person with less seniority. You are thrown into confusion, and no light seems to clear up the series of unexpected blows after being a faithful Christian for so many years. This is precisely where we must make that blind act of faith in Our Lord Jesus Christ; this is when our faith becomes so meritorious and rewarding in God's eyes. All of this is like a dark night of the soul.

3) Like the disciples of John the Baptist, we too are puzzled at

times, we feel like asking the same question: "Are You really the Messiah, the Christ who is to come into the world?"

4) It is precisely in the midst of this kind of darkness and doubt that we should prayerfully open the New Testament and read slowly and reflectively to let our Savior speak to us, to allay our doubts and assure us that it is He and we need not be afraid.

****

1) That the Lord increase our faith.

2) That we strive to strengthen our faith by daily reflection on the Gospels.

3) For all those who are honestly seeking the truth, that God in His mercy give them the light to see and the strength to embrace it.

4) For all those who are drifting and are in the throes of doubts and trials, that the Lord reaffirm them in their faith.

5) For an increase in vocations to the priesthood and religious life.

6) For the success of the ecumenical movement, that all Christians be one.

Thursday, Third Week of Advent: Lk. 7:24-30

I. Human history is calculated by the abbreviations B.C. and A.D., denoting years before and after Christ. Jesus then is the focal point of history. Our Lord Jesus Christ came to redeem us, to restore us to our favored but lost inheritance, and has raised us to the privileged relationship of sons and daughters to God the Father.

II. Jesus pays unique tribute to John the Baptist: "Of men born of women there is none greater than John the Baptist." John is the crowning point of the Old Testament. He is the bridge to the New Testament. He is the greatest figure of the Old Testament. Still he lacked what you and I have received, baptism of water and the Holy Spirit, which makes us sons and daughters of God in a new kingdom not yet established during John's lifetime.

III. John gives no evidence of comprehending the Christmas mystery. He believed that Jesus was the Messiah, but did not realize that Jesus was both God and man, God incarnate come to walk among us. He knew that the Messiah would be an exceedingly extraordinary individual, but he had no idea that the Messiah would be God come among us as a man. Jesus makes His identity known during the years of His public ministry.

1) Through Our Lord Jesus Christ, we are given more knowledge of God than was given to John or to the prophets.

2) Through baptism, we are literally made part of God by being ingrafted into His very nature and participate intimately in the divine life of the triune God.

IV. John the Baptist was the privileged forerunner and harbinger of the Messiah. Yet we have a greater privilege than John because we have heard the Good News of the Gospel (see Mt. 13:17). By living out its message we are brought into a very close relationship with Almighty God Himself.

1) Because of Our Lord Jesus Christ, we are members of a new creation inaugurated by Him. Like John, we too must be heralds of Christ by bringing His message into our spheres of activities so as to touch others with that message and dispose them to receive the gift of faith.

2) Our baptism confers upon us missionary obligations of evangelization. In our own modern but secular society many people have not been exposed to the Gospel, and to that extent they never felt the challenge of confronting, on a personal level, the person and message of Our Lord Jesus Christ. Unfortunately they are among our nation's millions of unchurched people, who really are sheep without a shepherd and who have not been adequately exposed to the good news of the Gospel. You and I must give them that exposure to Christ's message when we rub shoulders with them in the work world. The best exposure we can give them is by living that message in our everyday lives. The fruit of our example will exert a powerful influence in drawing them to Christ.

V. The Second Vatican Council stated: "All Christians by the example of their lives and the witness of the word, wherever they live, have an obligation to manifest the new man which they put on in baptism, and to reveal the power of the Holy Spirit by whom they were strengthened at confirmation, so that others, seeing their good works, might glorify the Father and more perfectly perceive the true meaning of human life and the universal solidarity of mankind" (*Ad Gentes*, Decree on the Church's Missionary Activity, No. 11).

1) "Whoever brings back a sinner from the error of his way will

save his soul from death and will cover a multitude of sins" (Jas. 5:20).

2) St. John Chrysostom said, "I can't believe in the salvation of anyone who does not work for the salvation of one's neighbor." He put such importance on zeal for souls that for him it was a greater thing to convert a sinner than to give all one's alms to the poor.

3) Let us remember that Christianity is advanced in the world not by churches becoming full of people but by people becoming full of Christ Jesus and bringing Him to others.

****

1) That we frequently express our gratitude to Almighty God for having sent His Son into the world to redeem us.

2) That God give us a zeal for souls, especially for those with whom we work or recreate.

3) That we pray frequently, especially for relatives and friends who have become indifferent or who have lost their faith.

4) That we be conscious of the effect of our example on others.

5) That we prepare for Christmas by a sincere sorrow for sin and a positive effort to do penance, especially by way of acts of charity.

6) That God fill us with a true and prudent zeal for souls.

7) For the success of the ecumenical movement, that all Christians be one.

Friday, Third Week of Advent: Jn. 5:33-36

I. "If I bear witness to myself, my testimony need not be accepted as true" (Jn. 5:31). By this thirty-fifth verse of the fifth chapter of the Gospel of St. John, Jesus is really citing a Jewish principle based on the Book of Deuteronomy, chapter 19, verse 15, which states: "A single witness shall not prevail against a man for any crime or for any wrong in connection with any offense that he has committed; only the evidence of two witnesses, or of three witnesses, shall the charge be sustained." Jesus accepts the Jewish principle that the evidence of one person cannot be taken as sufficient proof.

II. Jesus refers to the evidence that John gave as a lamp, "set aflame and burning bright," which gave the light of incontestable evidence inspired by God. John is the light which bore the testimony that Jesus is the Messiah.

1) Jesus observes, "For a time you were pleased to take pleasure in his light," meaning that John the Baptist was the sensation of the time, and as long as he said things that the scribes and Pharisees liked to hear he was listened to, but as soon as he spoke difficult truths or truths that tended to embarrass them, he was rejected.

2) How true this is of many people today. How they love a sermon that stimulates and thrills, but as soon as it targets in on a guilty conscience by touching the area of a sinful habit or an attachment to some immoral lifestyle or companionship, or on the delicate area of the immorality of the use of artificial contraception, then they don't want to hear such sermons.

III. Jesus refers to John, but does not plead for John's evidence on His behalf, for He says, "I have a greater testimony than John's — my works."

1) The old adage "Actions speak louder than words" can easily be applied convincingly to Jesus. "The works my Father has given me to do, these very works which I perform testify on my behalf." The works of Jesus are the compelling proofs of His messiahship. His miracles spoke a much more convincing testimony that the preaching of John the Baptist.

2) Jesus would continue to corroborate the message He has from His Father by many more miracles of spiritual and physical healings and finally by His most convincing miracle — His resurrection from the dead.

IV. Christ is the light; John is the lamp. John's mission was to point to the true light of the world, and Jesus would give living testimony by His compelling Gospel and His marvelous works.

1) The beauty of Jesus' message, His Gospel, is so compelling that it of itself is a convincing light that reveals His true identity as the Messiah and Savior. No more beautiful document has ever been written than the Gospel of Our Lord Jesus Christ. What a wonderful world we would be living in if men and women took it to heart and put it into practice. There would be no more wars.

2) Jesus' Gospel, if heeded, has the power to transform this world into a veritable heaven on earth. Alas, for those who do not

wish to see the light, Jesus becomes a contradiction and a two-edged sword which divides people either for or against Him.

3) All those who wish to follow Jesus and His Gospel will also become so many signs of contradiction, because their example will prick the consciences of weak, indulgent men and women who are living immoral lifestyles. Mother Teresa stings the consciences of the wealthy who hoard their resources, because her good work among the poor is a light and salt for those who know they are not doing near enough to alleviate the plight of the poor.

4) The Lord wants us to be light and salt to others, especially the weak, that they might turn on to God's moving grace and embrace the good news of His Gospel.

****

1) For all those who preach the word of God, that they may serve as true lights to the world.

2) For the Holy Father, bishops, and all authorities in the Church, that they may courageously proclaim the Gospel of social justice.

3) For all of those men and women who are working for social justice in the Third World, that they might see their sacrifices come to fruition.

4) For all people who have closed their eyes or ears to the Gospel because of some evil in their lives, that they be touched by the grace of repentance during this Advent season.

5) For peace in the world, and for an end to the arms race and to terrorism.

December 17 (if a weekday): Mt. 1:1-17

I. In recent years Americans have become more and more interested in finding their roots. We all like to know the history of our families. This knowledge helps us to ground ourselves in our own identities.

II. The Jewish people were very interested in genealogies, for they set great store on the purity of their lineage.

1) St. Matthew was writing his Gospel to the Jewish people and therefore he realized how important it would be at the outset of his Gospel to set forth the genealogy of Jesus to prove not only that He

was a descendent of Abraham but that He was also of the royal lineage of the house of King David.

2) The Messiah was prophesied to come forth from the house of David. Both Mary and Joseph were descendants of the house of David, but at that time genealogies were only given from the male line.

III. The genealogy is set forth in three groups of fourteen, and fourteen is a multiple of seven. Seven is considered to be the perfect number.

1) Creation is narrated in a seven-day episode. Thus the basic time unit of a week is divided into seven days.

2) Biblically speaking, seven symbolized totality or completeness (McKenzie, *Dictionary of the Bible*).

IV. Jesus fills the prerequisite conditions required of the Messiah. He is of Israelite stock that goes back to Abraham, and He is of David's offspring.

1) The first set of fourteen goes from Abraham down to David — the greatest of Israel's kings. The second set of fourteen generations brings us up to the period of the Babylonian exile, when King Jechoniah was taken captive with his people by the Babylonians in 587 B.C. The third set of fourteen generations takes us down to the birth of Jesus.

2) Each of these fourteen generations can be taken to be complete periods of Jewish history.

V. Contrary to custom, Matthew lists the names of four women in his genealogy. These include Rahab, who was a Canaanite prostitute; Tamar, who entered into an incestuous relationship with her father-in-law; Ruth, who was a foreigner from Moab and a non-Jewess; and Bathsheba, who entered into adultery with King David.

1) Even though Our Lord Jesus Christ was above sin, He is a descendent of sinners and foreigners. He would later be criticized for associating with sinners, Gentiles, and tax collectors.

2) This genealogy also symbolizes the universal mission of Jesus. Salvation is extended to all peoples, not only to the Jews but to the Gentiles or foreigners as well. Indeed it extended to the whole human family, all of whom are descendants of Adam and Eve.

3) Jesus would now be the new Adam, and Mary would be the

new Eve. Being of the blood lineage of Abraham would no longer be a condition for salvation as it was in the minds of the Jews. They believed that the Messiah was to be exclusively theirs. Jesus made it known that His mission was to the entire world.

4) Through baptism we become the new chosen people, the elect of the Father. How grateful we should feel for the magnificent gift of being not only sons and daughters of Abraham through faith, but sons and daughters of God the Father through the redemptive merits of Our Lord Jesus Christ!

5) God extends His love to the whole human race. Like the Jews of old, we are a chosen people. Now we can say that He loves each one of us with a particular and total love. Our Lord Jesus said to St. Margaret Mary that His love for us is such that if it were necessary He would suffer and die again to save one single soul. He said to her, "Behold the Heart that has loved men so much and is so little loved in return."

****

1) That we be mindful to express our gratitude to Almighty God for the gift of Our Lord Jesus Christ.

2) That we be grateful also for the gift of our heavenly Mother, the Blessed Virgin Mary.

3) That the narration of the genealogy of Our Lord make us mindful of the sacredness of marriage and of the Christian family.

4) That we always work in a special way for the salvation of the members of our own families.

5) That all couples who are experiencing difficulties in their marriages look to St. Joseph and Mary for the help and guidance they need, and that they be blessed with a genuine love for each other and a generous spirit of mutual sacrifice.

December 18 (if a weekday): Mt. 1:18-24

I. According to our way of thinking, it seems quite puzzling to learn of Joseph talking about divorce when he was not yet married to Mary. Sacred Scripture tells us that Joseph was espoused to Mary. In the Israel of that day, marriage involved three steps. First there was the engagement, and in many cases this was done by the couple's parents without the young man or woman having even seen each other. The betrothal confirmed or ratified the engagement. Up until the betrothal, the engagement could be broken and each party was free to seek another. But once the betrothal was entered into, it was absolutely binding. During the engagement and betrothal periods, the couple was called husband and wife but could not yet live together until they were formally married. The actual marriage took place at the end of the betrothal period, which lasted one year. This is when the young man came to take the young lady to their new home (W. Barclay, *The Gospel of Matthew*).

II. In today's Gospel narrative, Joseph and Mary were in the betrothal stage; that is, the committed stage.

1) For a young woman to become pregnant to another man during this stage would be considered adultery. Joseph was naturally perturbed, and being the honorable man that he was, he did not want to expose Mary, nor to denounce her. He could not bring himself to believe that she had committed adultery. In Jewish law, adultery was punishable by stoning.

2) In his great charity and magnificence, Joseph suspended judgment on Mary, so he decided to put her away quietly and not bother with the marriage as planned. While he was contemplating this whole unhappy procedure, an angel appeared to him in a dream to assure him that Mary's pregnancy was not the product of an adulterous affair; rather it was the work of the Holy Spirit, and Joseph was to give the child the name "Jesus," for He was the Promised One of Israel, the Emmanuel predicted by Isaiah, "the God Among Us." He would save His people from their sins.

III. St. Joseph gives us that striking example of magnanimity. Even in the face of what looked like convincing evidence against Mary, Joseph would not allow himself the freedom to pass judgment.

1) God's favor was shown to Jacob's son Joseph, because he refused to judge his brothers who had sold him to the Ishmaelites, who in turn sold him into slavery in Egypt. Joseph, instead of being vengeful of his brothers, wept when he saw them in Egypt in search of grain.

2) Our Lord Jesus Christ refused to pass judgment on the woman taken in adultery. He did not call Peter a perjurer, even though Peter had denied Him three times. He would not call Mary Magdalene an adulteress.

3) How attractive to Almighty God is the man or woman who has this Christlike magnanimity and largess — that even in the face of evidence that would lead to judgment, he/she would look to excuse rather than accuse another person. This assures a benign judgment from Almighty God.

4) Our Lord tells us, or rather warns us, "Judge not, and you will not be judged; condemn not, and you will not be condemned; forgive, and you will be forgiven; give, and it will be given to you. ... For the measure you give will be the measure you get back" (Lk. 6:37-38).

IV. What a beautiful sacrifice a person makes to God when he/she makes a positive effort against making harsh judgments of others. Such a one is a community builder. Such a positive effort to mortify one's tendency to critically judge others is very pleasing to Almighty God; it is worth more in God's eyes than many penances and prayers, for by such a practice one imitates the Son of God in the higher echelon of charity.

1) In his *Confessions*, St. Augustine writes of two basic vices in man: the tendency to be severe toward our neighbor, and the tendency to be indulgent toward ourselves. At the bottom of this is, of course, pride.

2) St. Francis de Sales was commissioned by the Holy See to restore peace and harmony to a monastery that was full of dissension and bitterness. Instead of waving threats and passing judgments on the culprits of the dissension, the saint broke down and cried during the course of his talk to the monks. He wept because Our Lord Jesus Christ was not being served there as the monks had committed themselves to do.

3) When we are tempted to pass judgment on another, let us strive to say with St. Philip Neri: "There, but for the grace of God, go I."

****

1) That we make the heroic effort not to pass judgment on others.
2) That we endeavor to defend the absent when they are being maligned or detracted.
3) That God give us the wisdom to see things the way He does.
4) That married couples not engage in suspicions or arguments,

but look to Joseph and Mary for inspiration to live in peaceful harmony.

5) For the diminution and cessation of violence in the world.

December 19 (if a weekday): Lk. 1:5-25

I. To be childless in the Jewish community was a catastrophe, and it was acceptable grounds for a divorce. Zechariah loved his wife, Elizabeth. She, like her husband, was a descendant of Aaron, the brother of Moses and the first high priest in Israel.

1) Zechariah pertained to the division of priests who descended from Abijah, of which there were eight hundred members, and duties were assigned to them by lot (Chautard, *Soul of the Apostolate*).

2) Only one priest could burn incense in the morning and evening of each day. The chances of serving on the altar were one in eight hundred. It so happened that the lot fell to Zechariah. We can imagine his ecstatic joy at this priestly privilege.

II. Zechariah's preoccupation was his family's disgrace: he and his wife, Elizabeth, were childless after many years of marriage. As he entered the court of the priests, his prayer must have been that the Lord take away the curse from his house and grant them a child.

1) As Zechariah was burning incense at the altar, the Archangel Gabriel appeared to him with the news that his prayers had been answered, and that his wife would bear him a son.

2) Zechariah did not believe the news that this great messenger of God brought to him, and because of his lack of belief, he was struck mute. He left the holy of holies unable to speak.

III. In spite of the great sign of the Archangel Gabriel's presence, Zechariah still doubted. His prayer lacked that filial trust which is so necessary for prayer, even in the face of an extraordinary sign — the presence of an archangel of the Lord.

1) So many of us pray in the same way as Zechariah: we pray for something, but in our hearts and souls we really do not believe that God will grant what we are asking. Generally this is due to a feeling of a lack of power in our prayer necessary to move God.

2) What this all boils down to is a real lack of faith and confidence in God's goodness and generosity. This type of prayer reduces itself to mere formality, going through the routine and

making the motions but not believing that our petition is going to be heard. This defeats our prayer before we even start.

3) We really might conclude from this Gospel narrative that Zechariah's prayers were not heard; it was rather the fervent prayer coming from the heart of his saintly wife, Elizabeth, that was heard.

IV. No doubt many of us have thought on occasion that if we had lived during the time of Our Lord's public ministry and could have been in the crowds who listened to Him speak and were able to have access to Him in order to ask Him personal favors, as the people did in fact do, He surely would have heard us and granted our petition. Those who were incapable of getting to Him, because of a paralysis or other debility, shouted out to Him to hear them or had others bring them to Him. With all of them the Lord was most compassionate and responsive.

1) The four Evangelists recounted many of the miracles the Savior did in fact work, but they failed to note the many persons Jesus refused because of their lack of faith or inadequate dispositions.

2) We are in messianic times; our Savior is very much with us in the Eucharist. How well the saints understood the healing power of Our Lord Jesus Christ in the Eucharist. St. Teresa of Ávila writes, "Now when Christ was in the world, the sick were cured by merely touching His garments; how can we doubt that He will heal us when He is within us [in Holy Communion] if we have faith? The Lord does not pay cheaply for His lodgings, if we show Him true hospitality!"

V. It was the woman behind the scenes that won the favor Zechariah was seeking. She, Elizabeth, was confident and persistent in her prayers. This is the only way we will ever get our prayers heard. Let us imitate this great woman of faith. "Confidence," says St. Bernard, "is only successful to the degree that it is daring in its hope." Let our hope be supported by unflagging persistence and confidence in our loving God.

****

1) That we learn to hope for great things from God.

2) That we be daring in our petitions and not give in to the weakness of thinking that the Lord won't give us what we ask of Him.

3) That we be quick to express our gratitude for all that the Lord has done for us.

4) That we go to Almighty God through the intercessory power of our heavenly Mother and the saints.

5) That we preface our petitions with a sincere act of contrition for our sins.

6) That the Lord increase our faith, our trust and confidence in Him.

December 20 (if a weekday): Lk.1:26-38

I. "Rejoice, O highly favored daughter. The Lord is with you. Blessed are you among women. . . . You have found favor with God." Two virtues shine in our Blessed Lady at the angelic salutation: her faith and her obedience.

1) Mary believed the message of the Archangel Gabriel. From then on, Mary believed that the child to be born was the Messiah, and in spite of the many trials awaiting her, she never doubted for a moment that her Son was the Messiah.

2) Her faith would be tried many, many times and often by difficult trials, but she never complained, doubted, or weakened in her firm belief.

3) Sacred Scripture records no miracles wrought by Jesus prior to His public ministry, so Mary saw no visible sign of her Son's divinity.

4) Her faith was tested from the very beginning: she had to give birth to the Christ Child in a stable because there were no accommodations for her in any of the inns of Bethlehem. Jesus worked no miracles to prevent King Herod from seeking to kill Him; rather Joseph and Mary had to flee to Egypt and seek refuge there in a land that was hostile to Jews. Mary lost her husband and had to live in poverty in Nazareth for many years. Finally she had to witness her Son's horrible death and listen to the insults, jeers, and blasphemies that the crowd hurled at her Son on the Cross.

5) Mary's faith is perhaps her greatest virtue. For it she has won the admiration of the whole Church; indeed she is, as the Second Vatican Council put it, the model the Church strives to emulate and become.

II. "I am the maidservant of the Lord. Let it be done to me as you say." Her obedience followed and was inspired by her faith. It was a spontaneous, cheerful, and generous obedience to the will of God under the cover of His divine providence. It involved very difficult trials. Her fidelity to the Lord's will pervaded her entire life. As it was with her Son, her meat was to do the will of the Father.

III. Mary can be considered the Ark of the New Testament; just as the Ark of the Covenant housed the Covenant of Mt. Sinai, the Ten Commandments, and the rod of Aaron, the first high priest of the Old Law, so too Mary housed the supreme High Priest in her womb, who is the final and most sacred covenant between God and the human race. Mary made it possible through the "yes" of her free consent for the eternal Word of God to become man.

IV. Faith and obedience go hand in hand. Indeed St. Teresa, a Doctor of the Church, writes, "One gets closer to God through obedience than through prayer." Our Lord Jesus Christ taught us in the Lord's Prayer that we pray that God's will be done on earth as it is in heaven. Heaven, in other words, is where His will is perfectly done. It follows logically then that the more earnestly we strive to know His will in our own lives and carry it out, the more we will be living a heavenlike life, and this even in the midst of sufferings and trials, because a deep, abiding inner joy will pervade the souls of those who really strive to know and do the Lord's will.

1) St. Gregory writes: "Obedience is the one virtue that inserts and engenders in the soul all other virtues, and after inserting them, preserves them" (Rodriguez, *Practice of Perfection and the Christian Virtues*).

2) The tremendous truth of Christianity is that in spite of how God longs that we carry out His will in our lives, He will never coerce us by force but will pursue us with love.

V. How can we know what God's will is for us?

1) Certain things are evident: the Ten Commandments for one, fidelity to our state and commitments in life, and obedience to the magisterium or teaching authority of the Church. This is expressed in conciliar documents and in the exhortations of the Holy Father. This is not always easy, but it is part of the "sweet yoke and light burden" our Savior spoke about.

2) In difficult areas, we should seek light and direction from our spiritual director or confessor. In our prayers we should always ask

55

for the light and knowledge to know God's will, as Our Lord instructed, and for the courage to carry it out cheerfully and faithfully. Its rewards are those two fruits of the Holy Spirit: peace and joy.

3) Let us have recourse to the Blessed Virgin Mary in our trials, mindful of the words of St. Bernard, "Nothing is given to us except through Mary, for such is the will of God. Just so, no one can come to the Supreme Father except the Son, so no one, almost no one can come to Christ except through Mary."

****

1) In all those areas where God's will is evident, may we always carry it out faithfully.

2) That the Lord give us the fortitude to carry out His will in spite of criticism and persecution.

3) That young people be steadfast in refusing to traffic in or to take drugs.

4) That all couples having difficulties in their marriages strive to make their marriages work by seeking out the help and the intercessory power of Joseph and Mary.

5) That through the intercession of the Blessed Virgin Mary we too may have a lively and deep faith.

6) That our Catholic people especially respect and honor the magisterium of the Church as it is expressed through the exhortations of our Holy Father.

December 21 (if a weekday): Lk. 1:39-45

I. By her words of consent, Mary becomes truly the dwelling place of God among men. Formerly, God's presence was symbolized by the Ark of the Covenant or by the Temple in Jerusalem. Now God dwells much more fully in the human person of Mary.

II. When Mary enters the house of Zechariah, Elizabeth bursts forth into a loud cry of joy and the infant John the Baptist leaps with joy in his mother's womb at the presence of the Lord.

1) David danced and leaped with joy around the Ark of the Covenant as he was having it brought from Abinadab's house in Baalah of Judah to Jerusalem where it was to have permanent residence in the future temple to be built by Solomon. King David

danced with joy because the Ark symbolized the presence of God among His people.

2) So now, the infant, John the Baptist, leaps with joy in the presence of his Lord and God. In the meeting of these two infants, the Old Testament meets the New Testament, and John, the last of the Old Testament prophets, begins his role of identifying the Savior, a role he would climax in the Jordan, where he would point out Jesus as the Lamb of God who was to take away the sins of the world.

III. As Christmas approaches, we too, like St. Elizabeth and John the Baptist, should be filled with joy. Why? Because we are a privileged people; we are the children of God; Jesus Christ is our Redeemer and Brother; He has opened the gates of heaven to us and has given us the means of getting there.

IV. Like Mary, we too are the temples of the Holy Spirit, and the kingdom of God is within us. This should be the cause of our joy.

1) Joy is the consequence of the possession of a desired good. The more valuable the object, the more ecstatic the joy upon acquiring that good.

2) Joy is not a virtue; it is a fruit of love — the love that generously gives of itself to serve God through others, this love is manifested exteriorly through sacrificial service to our brothers and sisters.

3) The good, loving, and faithful Christian possesses Jesus Christ, the highest possible good. Hence, Our Lord Jesus Christ is the cause of his/her joy, The essence of that joy is the presence of God within the soul. As a consequence, that soul is filled with enthusiasm for God and the things of God. The word "enthusiasm" comes from the Greek words "en" and "theos," meaning God within. It is the possession of God within one that causes immense joy.

V. When Brother Elias told St. Francis of a dream he had about him, that Francis was going to die in two years, this news filled Francis with joy because he was going to see fully the One who already dwelt in his heart: Our Lord Jesus Christ.

1) Faith makes us more aware of Christ's presence within us. As our faith grows, so too will the realization of Christ's presence within us intensify, and so too will our joy be so much the greater because of it.

2) No more does God dwell in temples of stone, brick, and

mortar, but in the baptized. Like Mary, every Christian should be a sign of God's presence in the world.

3) Mary was united to God in perfect obedience: "Behold the handmaid of the Lord, be it done unto me as you will." God's presence in us will be more evident the more we conform our wills to His.

4) When we cooperate with His graces and inspirations, we become more like Him. Then with Mary we too can say, "The Lord has done great things for me."

5) With John the Baptist and Elizabeth, we too have reason to praise God, since He loves us so much that He has given us His Son to dwell within us and abide with us in the sacrament of the Eucharist.

6) As we prepare to receive Our Lord in the Eucharist, let our hearts be filled with the humility and the gratitude of St. Elizabeth as we too say with gratitude and humility: "Who am I that my Lord should come to me?"

****

1) That God may give us a deeper and more lively faith that will make us realize more realistically that Christ dwells within us, and thus that we may be filled with a greater joy.

2) That we be more generous in cooperating with the graces and inspirations of the Holy Spirit, that the presence of Christ within us be more evident to others and thus inspire them to lead better lives.

3) That we prepare with anticipation for the reception of Our Lord Jesus Christ in the Eucharist, and make adequate thanksgiving after receiving this precious sacrament.

4) That our Christian joy be more manifest to others.

5) For peace in the world and an end to terrorism and to the arms race.

December 22 (if a weekday): Lk. 1:46-56
I. The Magnificat or Canticle of Mary is chanted every evening in monasteries and religious communities throughout the world. It is a song of joyful praise and deep gratitude to God for His goodness and mercy.

II. The Magnificat contains the elements of perfect prayer: praise, adoration, thanksgiving, reparation, and petition.

III. Mary personifies her people, Israel, and she becomes their mouthpiece to praise and thank God, for the long-expected One is now to come into the world. Mary sings this song of gratitude because the Messiah has deigned to come into the world and that she has been selected to be God's instrument in bringing Him into the world. Her Magnificat is a hymn of joyful gratitude, of acceptance, and of appreciation that God has selected her to serve as God's instrument in bringing the Savior into the world. It is a hymn of joyful obedience and disposal of herself to the will of God. It is at the same time a penitential hymn, because Mary disposes herself to sacrifice herself at whatever the cost or suffering her acceptance of this special mission might bring her. She will serve as a vessel of reparation and become the co-redemptrix in the redemptive mission of her Son.

IV. The last part of her Canticle recalls the promise made to Abraham; and Mary, a descendant of Abraham, is the person in whom God's promise reaches its fulfillment. This hymn of praise singles out God's preference for the humble and the poor who constitute the privileged section of the messianic people.

1) God scatters the proud and brings their plans to confusion, because they arrogate something to themselves that really belongs to God. The Canticle tells us that the beginning of any meaningful relationship with God Himself must be based on humility, sincerity, and openness to Him to do His holy will.

2) Mary tells us, as Christ Himself will reiterate repeatedly, that God exalts the humble and casts down the proud.

V. This prayer of Mary touches God's favor for the poor and lowly. "He fills the hungry with good things" and sends away empty those who are selfishly tied to their importance or wealth.

1) Quoting Isaiah, the Son of Mary will say, "He has sent me to preach the good news to the poor," the food that truly fills, nourishes, and satisfies, and that food is the word of God.

2) Like Mary, we too must become godlike in our attitude toward the lowly and the poor. Christianity cannot tolerate a situation where some have too much of this world's goods and others do not have enough to live on in dignity. Christianity's virtue par excellence

is charity, that sensitivity toward others which urges us to share with those in need.

3) God will show His favor to us if we show favor to those in need, for Christ insists that whatever we do even to the least of our brothers and sisters we do to Him (Mt. 25:40).

4) Wealth or social class does not court favor with Almighty God, since Christ has died for all without exception, thus raising us to a classless society or a society of equals before Him who favors neither rank nor bankbook; yet His predilection is with the poor.

5) We all must manifest equal dependence on Him for everything, but above all for our sanctification and salvation.

6) Today, then, with Mary let our hearts be filled with gratitude at the good things the Lord has done for us, and not be envious of those who may have more talent or more of this world's goods. Greater responsibility is demanded of those who happen to be stewards of more talent or more wealth. With Mary, let us praise God and be grateful for whatever we may possess, be it talent or wealth, and like Mary let us be instruments in God's hands for the extension of His kingdom to the minds and hearts of all men and women and sedulously work for the sanctification and salvation of souls.

VI. May Mary's Magnificat remind us to always be at God's disposal, to be constantly preparing ourselves for His use when He deigns to call upon us to serve as His instruments in extending His kingdom here on this earth. The Magnificat echoes the words of the "Our Father": "Thy kingdom come, Thy will be done on earth as it is in heaven."

****

1) For an increase in fervent devotion to the blessed Virgin Mary.

2) That we be mindful to render daily praise and thanksgiving to God for all His benefits, but especially for the gift of His divine Son to us.

3) That we be more diligent in the work of our own sanctification, that the Lord find in us more suitable and apt instruments for the extension of His kingdom on earth.

4) That we be generous to the lowly and the poor.

5) That God reward us with the rich gift of humility.

6) For an end to the arms race, and that more money previously used for armaments be given to alleviate world poverty.

7) That we may always feel the protection of the Blessed Virgin Mary throughout life, and especially at the moment of our death.

December 23 (if a weekday): Lk. 1:57-66

I. The unusual circumstances surrounding the birth of John the Baptist and the conferral of a name different from his father's or his ancestors were all so many signs of the uniqueness of this child and his future mission.

II. From Shakespeare's Romeo and Juliet comes the famous question: "What's in a name? That which we call a rose by any other name would smell as sweet." In biblical times, unlike our present day, names had rich meaning. They expressed gratitude, an answer to a prayer, joy, fervor, mission, etc. In Hebrew culture, a name is thought to tell something of the kind of person the bearer of that name is (McKenzie, *Dictionary of the Bible*).

1) Samuel, the Old Testament Judge, was the product of his mother's prayers after years of marriage, and it means, "he over whom the name of God is pronounced." Elijah means "Jehovah is my God."

2) In the Hebrew mentality, a person's name was to reveal much of the nature or character of that person. John's name means "the Lord has shown favor."

3) A change in a personal name indicated a change in the person; thus, God changed Abram's name to Abraham. A covenant was struck, leaving Abram with new responsibilities. He was a new person in his relation to God and his own people.

III. John the Baptist was the greatest of the prophets, for not only was he to speak about the coming of the Messiah but it devolved upon him to point the Messiah out to the people.

IV. Zechariah's tongue had been silenced when he doubted the archangel's message. It would not be loosened until he would make a strong act of faith. He professed this faith and trust in God's message by insisting upon giving the child his heavenly-ordained name.

1) When he wrote, "J-O-H-N is his name," his tongue was loosened, and John, which means "the Lord has shown favor," was

God's instrument to show favor to Zechariah. John's father then received his ability to speak.

2) Zechariah, which means "the Lord has remembered," saw realized the faithful promise of the Lord to grant him a son.

V. It was on the eighth day that Jewish boys were circumcised and given their names. Girls could be named within thirty days after their birth. Elizabeth means "the Lord has sworn." She, like Hannah, the mother of Samuel, the prophet and outstanding figure in Israel's history, prayed so hard for a child that she was rewarded for her faith and perseverance in prayer. Her name implies that God is faithful, and the Lord did grant her request.

VI. It was in the enforced silence imposed upon Zechariah when he was left speechless that he reflected prayerfully on the Archangel Gabriel's message.

1) He too had prayed for a son, and as his name signifies, "the Lord has remembered," the Lord granted his request. More likely the request was granted through the persistent prayer of faith of his wife, Elizabeth.

2) The greatest gift to any home is a child; it is the cause of parents' joy. John the Baptist was a joy to his parents, as Jesus was to Joseph and Mary.

VII. Names are important, and they should be reflected upon and thought out, and not hastily bestowed. As with our biblical counterparts, a name should say something about the person upon whom it is bestowed.

1) Some parents give the wildest and strangest names to their children. They are named after soap-opera characters or after actors and actresses instead of saints or biblical figures.

2) A saint's name can be evoked as a committed helper of the person bearing that saint's name, and the child might hopefully be urged to develop a devotion to that saint early on in life. The child should be introduced to the biography of his/her namesake, and this might be read to him/her by the child's parents. We all should remember to call upon our saintly namesakes for help and protection, and to cultivate a devotion to them.

****

1) That young people be generous in their marriages and have as many children as they can reasonably afford.

2) That parents be selective in giving baptismal names to their children.

3) That parents teach their children from their youngest years how to pray and to be familiar with their patron saints.

4) For all young couples who are having difficulties in their marriages, that their hurts may be healed.

5) That parents be conscious of their example before their children.

December 24 (morning): Lk. 1:67-79

I. There are similarities in the Benedictus (Canticle of Zechariah) and the Magnificat (Canticle of Mary). Both are full of Old Testament references and praise God for visiting His people.

II. The first part of the Benedictus is much like the prayers used in the Jewish circumcision ceremonies. It is full of the praises of the Lord for His goodness, His protection, and for visiting His people. Because He visits His people and fulfills His promises, the Benedictus urges us "to serve Him devoutly, and through all our days be holy in His sight." The second part addresses the newly circumcised John the Baptist. It is full of hope and optimism. The aspirations and hopes of the patriarchs, the prophets, and the people are now to be realized through the Messiah. John is to prepare the people for the proximate coming of the Messiah.

III. John the Baptist was to be the Elijah spoken of by the prophet Malachi, for he was the one who was to prepare the way of the Lord, as Zechariah is inspired to say in his canticle, the Benedictus. All devout Jews prayed, hoped, and longed for the coming of the Messiah. The dawn of salvation was breaking with John the Baptist. John was the lamp; Christ is the light. John was the horizon; Christ the mature sun, whose rays were now breaking in the person of John.

IV. The Benedictus specifies John's mission as one of preparation. He is to give the people knowledge of salvation and how to attain the remission of their sins.

1) This would be the same mission Our Lord Jesus Christ would

give to His Apostles: preach a fuller knowledge of God as taught by Christ, and the remission of sins through baptism.

2) This would in fact be the basic mission of the Church also. As her members, it should be our mission too.

V. The Benedictus canticle celebrates the fulfillment of the promises made to the patriarchs and of the prophecies made by Israel's great prophets.

1) The Messiah is called the "Horn of Salvation" and the "rising sun." He will deliver us from our sins and from the power of Satan and evil.

2) "His light will shine on those who sit in darkness and in the shadow of death to guide our feet into the way of peace." The first fruit of the Savior is peace. It was the message conveyed to the shepherds on the Judean hillsides at the birth of the Lord. It was our Savior's greeting to His Apostles each time He appeared to them after His resurrection: "Peace be to you."

VI. The Benedictus is a doxology of praise, of gratitude, and of hope.

1) It tells us of God's fidelity, of His faithfulness to His promises to us human beings.

2) All of this so marvelously shows just how merciful He will be toward those who really turn to Him with a life committed to be faithful to Him.

3) To His faithful ones He will give His peace and joy because He will give them His Son, who will dwell in their hearts.

VII. The Benedictus is a prayer of optimism and hope, a prayer that is full of anticipation for the coming of the Holy One of Israel — the Messiah and Savior.

1) For all Christians the Messiah and Savior did come into the world, and John the Baptist introduced Him to his followers as the "Lamb of God" who was to take away the sins of the world.

2) The Benedictus is still a prayer of hope and optimism for each individual Christian just as it was for the Jews who were longing for the coming of the "anointed one of Israel." For Christians, it is a longing for Christ's particular coming to them to carry them off to eternity.

3) For the truly spiritual person, Christ is the Spouse of the

human soul, and he/she eagerly awaits the coming of the divine Bridegroom to carry him/her off to the wedding banquet of eternity.

4) In a wider sense, the Benedictus looks also to the Parousia, or final coming of the Messiah at the end of time.

****

1) As an immediate preparation for Christmas, that we all recommit ourselves to serve God the best we can in our daily lives.

2) That the Lord fill us with a lively expectancy, hope, and joy this Christmastide.

3) That we strive to make the message of Christmas one of hope, peace, and joy by conveying this message in our daily lives, especially through the practice of charity toward our needy brothers and sisters.

4) That we strive to carry the warmth of Christmas to the lonely, the elderly, and to shut-ins.

5) That the Lord grant unity to His Church by bringing all Christian communities together.

6) For an end to the arms race and peace in the world.

7) That the message of Christ reach all those who are truly hungering for the truth.

CHRISTMASTIDE

I. St. Stephen was the first to fulfill the prophecy of Our Lord Jesus Christ: that is, that persecution and martyrdom would be the lot of missionaries who endeavor to spread the good news of the Gospel.

1) They would literally be sheep sent among wolves. To draw the analogy from the animal kingdom, the disciples should not "throw themselves to the wolves" of the world; rather, like the prudent serpent, they should be on their guard for such ravenous wolves, and avoid unnecessary conflict with them. The true disciple of Christ must walk the road of simplicity and prudence.

2) As with so much of the Christian paradox, persecution will draw the bearers of the Good News into a deeper relationship with the Lord.

II. Jesus said that brother would hand over brother to death; children would turn against their parents and have them put to death because of the two-edged-sword quality that would be so characteristic of the Gospel. Whoever holds out to the end, Jesus promised, would receive the crown of eternal life.

1) Jesus warns that His Gospel will be the cause of divisions even in the family. This was eminently so during the early centuries of the Church in the Roman Empire, where pagan parents or brothers or sisters would react violently against each other because one of them converted to Christianity.

2) This is one of the reasons why Christianity was such a persecuted religion in the Roman Empire, because it was the cause of so many divisions in Roman families.

III. Our Lord Jesus Christ would never water down His Gospel message to win over converts. When He preached the doctrine of the Eucharist, the crowds drifted away. It was too hard for them to accept, especially the notion of eating His Body and drinking His Blood. That was unacceptable to the Jewish mentality, because they were strictly forbidden to drink the blood of the animals offered in sacrifice on the altar of the Temple. The notion of partaking of blood was abhorrent.

1) Even His disciples walked away because they, too, found this doctrine of eating His Flesh and drinking His Blood too much.

2) When finally only His Twelve Apostles remained after the others drifted away, Jesus asked them, "Will you also go away?"

Peter answered for the rest: "Lord to whom shall we go? You have the words of eternal life" (Jn. 6:67-68).

IV. No, Our Lord Jesus Christ will not force us to accept His message, but He will give us the strength to bear witness to His Gospel, as St. Stephen fearlessly did even in the face of death.

1) St. Stephen was a heroic witness, and the first person to lay down his life for the cause of the Gospel. The shedding of his blood no doubt won the graces necessary for the conversion of Saul of Tarsus (the future St. Paul) to Christianity. St. Paul became the greatest missionary of Christianity.

2) The Acts of the Apostles says that Stephen was filled with grace and power, and that he worked wonders among the people. He was filled with such wisdom that he was no easy prey for those who disputed with him. As a result they trumped up charges of blasphemy against him, a crime that was punishable by stoning according to the Mosaic Law. False witnesses were brought in against him (Acts 6:8-15).

3) The blood of martyrs is the seed of Christianity, and St. Stephen was that first seed that bore such magnificent fruit, especially in the person of St. Paul the Apostle.

4) St. Stephen died with his eyes fixed trustingly on God in heaven together with a prayer of forgiveness on his lips. Like his Lord and Master, Our Lord Jesus Christ, he died begging forgiveness for his persecutors and executioners. He died fearlessly proclaiming the Gospel. May he win for us similar faith, zeal, and courage.

****

1) That we be true living witnesses of the Gospel to the world in which we live.

2) That the Lord bless us with prudence and simplicity.

3) That the Lord bless His Church with generous vocations.

4) That we more actively defend the lives of the unborn.

5) May the work of evangelization bring all Christians back into unity so that we might be one flock under one pastor.

6) For peace in the world and an end to terrorism.

December 27 (if a weekday): Jn. 20:2-8

I. In his own Gospel, John refers to himself as "the disciple whom Jesus loved." He was privileged to recline at the side of the Jesus at the Last Supper. No doubt, Jesus loved him deeply.

II. Of all the disciples, John alone stood with Mary beneath the Cross. It was through John that Jesus gave the Blessed Virgin Mary to the human race as its mother as He was dying on the Cross.

III. John's Gospel is different from that of the other Evangelists. He did not begin with the genealogy of Jesus as Matthew did, precisely because John wanted to emphasize that Jesus proceeded directly from God and not from human origin. John emphasizes the divinity of Jesus. Christ's human nature, though real and important, was secondary.

1) John's Gospel was written around the end of the first century, perhaps in the year 100. It was written well after the other Evangelists had written their Gospel accounts, perhaps some thirty to forty years after. It can well be assumed that John had full knowledge of the other Gospels, and for this reason he wrote his Gospel differently in order to add much to what was already written and thus enrich the Church with his wonderful and mystic insights into the life and message of Our Lord Jesus Christ.

2) His Gospel is more enriched for having known the Blessed Virgin better than the other Apostles. Jesus confided His mother to him until her death and assumption into heaven. We can only imagine the conversations that went on between John and Mary and how they have enriched his Gospel and Epistles.

IV. John is symbolized by the eagle because he soars upward with his mystic eye and penetrates into the profound truths of the Gospel. His deep understanding of divine things is reflected in what he wrote.

1) Burning with love and zeal, he possessed an intense inner longing that every person should come to know Jesus.

2) It is precisely at Christmas that we see the Son of God revealing Himself as man, beginning that marvelous work whereby we might share in His divinity and be raised up to the stature of sons and daughters of God our Father in heaven.

V. In today's Gospel narration, there is evidence to believe that John, the beloved disciple, did not seem to have believed or have expected the resurrection of Jesus from the dead. Upon seeing the empty tomb, however, he recalled what Jesus had said and immediately believed.

1) How earthbound were the thoughts of the Apostles even after having seen and heard Jesus say and do so much! It is proof that they, like us, needed the Holy Spirit in order to understand, and understanding, in this sense, is impossible without the gift of the Holy Spirit.

2) All the study in the world will never increase our faith; it is a sheer and gratuitous gift of God. We can never pray enough for it. A frequent ejaculation for all of us should be: "Lord, increase my faith." With an increase of faith comes an automatic increase in the gifts of the Holy Spirit.

VI. In his first letter to the Corinthians, St. Paul tells us that "God has revealed this wisdom to us through the Holy Spirit. The Spirit scrutinizes all matters even the deep things of God" (1 Cor. 2:10). It is through the Spirit that we come to understand and appreciate the things of God and long to be with Him in paradise.

1) The Spirit abides in us, prodding us on to a deeper understanding, knowledge, and appreciation of the revelation of Jesus Christ to the members of His Mystical Body, the Church.

2) This same Spirit of God inspires us and moves us to pray and praise God. The word "inspire" literally means "in-spirit" or in the Spirit. It is He who moves us to think, to love, and to do. He gives us a new vision with His sevenfold gifts.

VII. John is a seraphic lover of God. When intellects are incapable of understanding, love becomes the interpreter, and often it cannot put into words the object of its love. Love can grasp, embrace, and cleave to eternal truths when the intellect is left groping in the dark. John's message is one of love as that which best sums up the whole law and which, more than understanding, unites us to Our Lord Jesus Christ.

****

1) That God bless us with a deeper faith.

2) That we pray frequently to the Holy Spirit for the gift of wisdom and understanding, that we might appreciate more and more the things of God in order to be motivated to love Him more and more.

3) Like this great Apostle, St. John, may we too come to ever deeper love of God and our neighbor.

4) That we cultivate a love for Sacred Scripture and use it in our meditative prayer and as our refuge in the time of trial.

December 28 (if a weekday): Mt. 2:13:-18

I. Murder for King Herod was among the ordinary chores of his reign. No one was ever safe, not even the members of his own household. He had Mariamme, his second wife, and her mother, Alexandra, put to death. He had his three sons — Antipater, Alexander, and Aristobulus — tried and executed on charges of conspiracy. Herod was only half Jewish; yet he succeeded in winning the throne of Judaea from the Romans by his astuteness and his success in eliminating his opposition. Herod was ruthless and ambitious. He exterminated the members of the Sanhedrin (the High Court of the Jews), and he had some three hundred court officers put to death.

II. Anyone who constituted a threat to his throne was courting the danger of becoming another one of his many imprisoned or slaughtered victims.

1) When King Herod learned from the wise men about the birth of a newborn King in Judaea, the idea of a "threat" to his throne immediately seized him and filled him with the desire to eliminate the "Rival."

2) When he was tricked by the wise men, who did not return to inform him of the whereabouts of the newborn King, he put out the order to have all male children two years old and under put to death in order to be sure that he would have the new King eliminated.

III. When the Israelites constituted a threat to Pharaoh in Egypt, because of their increasing numbers, Pharaoh ordered the slaughter of all male infants.

1) The Hebrew child who was hidden in a basket and floated out on the Nile turned out to be the man who would lead the Israelites out of slavery across the Red Sea on their way to a new life in the promised land of Israel.

2) So too Our Lord Jesus Christ escaped Herod's slaughter to become the Savior of all mankind and to lead us to the promised land of paradise.

IV. It no longer takes mandates from kings and pharaohs to slaughter the innocent. Babies while in their mothers' wombs are ordered killed by their own mothers. In the cities of New York and Washington, D.C., more babies are aborted than are born alive. This cries out to heaven for vengeance.

1) Great people who were saved from the threat of abortion went on to make great contributions to mankind. Ludwig von Beethoven was one such child whose mother was counseled to abort her child by her doctor. She refused, and the world is still reaping the fruit of her steadfast decision.

2) The Second Vatican Council stated: "From the moment of its conception life must be guarded with the greatest care, while abortions and infanticide are unspeakable crimes" (*Church in the Modern World*, No. 51).

V. Today's feast of the Holy Innocents pricks the consciences of good men and women. It makes us aware of this great slaughter of innocent children who literally are being baptized in their own blood. It serves notice that we must strive and work to overcome this horrible killing of the innocent. To remain indifferent or distant in the matter of trying to reverse the Supreme Court's 1973 decision to allow abortions to take place in our country is to be guilty of omission. In the face of such evil, it would be morally wrong and remiss if good men and women did nothing about it. We all should lend moral and material support to genuine pro-life organizations that are working so hard to have the Supreme Court decision permitting abortion reversed. Similar support should be given to those pro-life groups who finance prenatal care, birth, and adoption expenses of infants whose innocent lives would otherwise be ruthlessly terminated by abortion.

****

1) That our nation will put an end to its murderous abortions.

2) That married couples accept with joy the children God sends them.

3) That those who must limit their families do not resort to the use of contraceptives, but resort to natural family planning which is good and permissible.

4) That children find in their parents the love, warmth, and security they need.

5) That runaways may find safe refuge, and above all that they find faith.

6) That the Covenant House project for runaways meets with continued success.

December 29 (if a weekday): Lk. 2:22-35

I. St. Luke mentions two important ceremonies in this passage: the rite of circumcision and the rite of purification.

1) On the eighth day after His birth, a male child was to be circumcised. Through this rite Jesus is formally inscribed in the community of God's chosen people.

2) The rite of purification is explained in chapter 12 of the book of Leviticus. Moses prescribed that for forty days after a woman gave birth to a male child, she was considered unclean. She was to go to the temple and bring a lamb for a holocaust and a young pigeon as a sacrifice for sin. If she could not afford a lamb, two turtledoves would suffice for the purification ceremony.

3) The priest was to perform the rite of atonement over her, and the woman was considered purified. Mary was unable to afford the lamb, so she brought the offering of the poor — two pigeons.

II. These ceremonies impressed upon the minds of the people the importance of a child born to a young couple as being indeed a great gift of God. Moreover, the firstborn male child was to be consecrated to God (Ex. 13:2).

1) A child is a great gift that God bestows on any couple and a source of joy to them. Nevertheless, even though the child is born to them, it still basically belongs to God.

2) Belonging basically to God, and at the same time being lent to a couple, places a great responsibility on the parents to rear that child in the faith, cultivating in him/her a knowledge and love of God.

III. Simeon was part of that devout, believing Jewish community which was expecting the coming of the Messiah. With deep faith and perseverance he prayed that God would permit him to see the Messiah before his death.

1) His prayers were granted. He receives the infant Jesus in his arms and sings the "Nunc dimittis," a hymn which is sung as part of

75

the Church's night prayer. Then he prophesies about Jesus and His mother, how the infant would become a sign of contradiction for Israel, and that Mary's soul would be pierced with the sword of suffering. The prophecy is valid for all faithful followers of Our Lord Jesus Christ.

2) Simeon says that Jesus would be the cause of the rise and fall of many in Israel. He would be the cause and the power that would free those caught in the bondage of the devil and sin.

3) At the same time, Jesus would be the cause of the fall of others — of the proud; those who would choose to remain in darkness and who would find His Gospel message disturbing.

4) Jesus would be a sign of contradiction. With Jesus, men and women would have to declare themselves, for there would be no neutral ground regarding Jesus: one would perforce accept or reject Him. For those who would accept, victory would be theirs; for those who would reject Him, condemnation awaited them.

IV. A sword would pierce Mary's soul. She would have to suffer much because of her Son. Mary would experience the seven dolors: from the flight into Egypt in order to escape Herod, to witnessing her Son's passion and death.

1) In God's plan, Mary is the personification of Israel. She is what the Church aspires to be. It is through her sufferings, the mystery of the contradiction of the Cross, that her faith is brought to consummate perfection.

2) So too for all Christians going through life, it is the trials and the crosses, those blows of life that bring our faith to maturity. In Mary we have a wonderful model and a compassionate mother who is willing to help us and to whom we should have confident and frequent recourse.

****

1) That the Lord deepen and increase our faith.

2) That all parents accept lovingly all the children that God sends them.

3) That parents take seriously their responsibility of instructing their children in the faith.

4) That God give to fathers and mothers the tact and the prudence to counsel and guide their children.

5) That parents engender in their children a deep devotion to the Blessed Virgin Mary, and teach them to go to her in time of trial and crisis.

December 30 (if a weekday): Lk. 2:36-40

I. In today's Gospel sketch, St. Luke narrates how one of the faithful remnant of Yahweh, a devout, prayerful old woman eighty-four years of age, grew in faith and hope with the passage of the years. She, like all good Jewish men and women, prayed for the coming of the Messiah and, no doubt like Simeon, hoped to see Him with her own eyes before departing this life.

II. She had been a widow for many years and nourished herself on continual prayer and meditation on the Scriptures. Because of her deep faith and persistent prayer, God became the companion of her widowhood.

1) Being alone can make people bitter and resentful, especially after the death of a loved one. The sorrows, trials, and loneliness of widowhood often make old men and women resentful, or, as in the case of Anna, it affords them with so much more time for God and the things of God. Anna used her solitude well; it actually made her youthful in hope and firmer in her faith.

2) God permitted the death of her husband, and probably she was without children; nevertheless, instead of being spiteful and vindictive toward God or cold toward Him, she turned toward Him as a Father, knowing that He would provide. The passage of the years did not weaken her hope in the coming of the Messiah, the Promised One who would redeem Israel.

III. Anna was a prophetess, a title given to other outstanding holy women of the Old Testament like Sarah, Deborah, Esther, Judith, and others. Here "prophetess" denotes her dedication to the temple liturgy and her prayerful and frequent meditation on Sacred Scripture (Thierry and Maertens). Like Simeon, Anna too would recognize and proclaim Jesus to be the Expected One of Israel.

IV. The Book of Deuteronomy (17:6) required that truth be established by two reliable witnesses. St. Luke has carefully made sure in writing the outstanding events of the life of Christ that these truths be attested to by at least two credible witnesses.

1) Anna's proclamation is true because she is reliable: a devout

and upright widow for many years who constantly spent her time in the temple in prayer and worship. Her character was impeccable.

2) Simeon is the primary witness, the faithful priest who served the temple with dedication. He probably endured much suffering and disappointment at having to witness the priestly betrayal of many priests of their sacred duties (Chautard). St. Luke calls him "just and pious."

3) Both Anna and Simeon become exemplary and credible witnesses to testify to the presence of the Messiah. Upon seeing the infant Jesus, Anna burst out in thanksgiving and went about proclaiming Him to be the long-awaited Messiah.

V. The word "widow" comes from Sanskrit and means "empty," a rather harsh description of such women. It is estimated that three out of every four married women will become widows. One out of six women over twenty-one is a widow (*Pulpit Resource*).

VI. Anna is an admirable example of old age. Though old in body, she was young in mind and spirit. She used her time not in gossiping but in prayer and meditation.

1) She was not forlorn because of her widowhood; her faith in God's providence was too strong to permit that. She never separated herself from the temple community; she remained a faithful, worshiping member.

2) How much less lonely old people would feel if they spent much of their time in prayer and meditation, being involved as much as possible in their church's activities in whatever way possible. Their faith, hope, prayers, and example can do so much to encourage young people, who themselves must project into the future to envision the possibility of finding themselves in a similar situation.

****

1) That the elderly find solace and comfort in frequent prayer and reflection on Sacred Scripture.

2) That old people in their limited capacity strive to be involved in the church community as much as possible.

3) That we think of the elderly frequently and visit them, especially our own relatives.

4) That widows may, like Anna, feel comforted and assured by a strong faith in the providence of God.

5) That those in charge of the elderly treat them with kindness, compassion, understanding, and dignity.

6) That the apostolate of the old be the salvation of the young.

December 31 (if a weekday): John 1:1-18

I. Light and life are two basic themes in John's Gospel. He opens his Gospel with the theme of Jesus being the light and life of men, and he closes his Gospel with the plea that we "believe that Jesus is the Christ the Son of God, and that believing you may have life in his name" (Jn. 20:31).

II. "I am the light of the world" (Jn. 8:12). "I have come that they might have life and have it more abundantly" (Jn. 10:10).

1) Jesus is the light that expels the darkness (Jn. 1:5). Only Jesus can make life worth living and give it its fullest and richest meaning.

2) Indeed it is the will of the Father that everyone who accepts Jesus and believes in Him should have life (Jn. 6:40). Through Jesus, we enter into the very life of God.

III. "I," said Our Divine Lord, "am the light of the world; he who follows me will not walk in darkness but will have the light of life" (Jn. 8:12). Jesus is that light of faith which illumines the path through the world that leads to happiness and eternal life. St. Augustine wrote that through Our Lord Jesus Christ, God intended to "show us the way by which He would lead us to the goal He had promised. It was not enough for God to give us His Son merely to point out the way. He made His Son Himself the Way, so that you might journey with Him as your guide, as He walks in His own way" (Orchard et al., ed., "Commentary on the Psalms").

1) Filled with a committed faith in Him, each of us will serve as a light that will illuminate the way for others, that will lead them to Our Lord. Just as a candle consumes itself in giving light, so too the Christian should spend him/herself in giving the light of witness to the Gospel for others to see.

2) St. Thomas Aquinas begged God to enlighten him as he prayed: "Cast a beam of Your radiance upon the darkness of my mind and dispel from me the double darkness of sin and ignorance in which I live." For Christians, to live one's life without Christ is to live in darkness and despair. We should never cease asking the Holy

Spirit to illuminate our minds and hearts and to fill us with the fire of His light and love.

3) The light of Christ is the light of faith which enlarges one's vision to look beyond the confining things and circumstances of this life and enables us to see the things that are unseen; that is, the eternal truths that give life.

IV. John the Baptist was to bear witness to the light. This he did in a humble and courageous way. This too is the vocation of every Christian.

1) In every age there are great witnesses who give testimony to what Christ has done for them, the miracles He has worked for them, or the meaning and direction He has given to their lives.

2) This has been the case with the multitudes of martyrs of all centuries, including our own, and of the many men and women who live out their faith quietly yet heroically as burning lights in a secular and hedonistic world.

V. In the final analysis, faith, that marvelous light of true wisdom, is a gift of God Himself. Without its light, one cannot recognize Jesus for who He really is. Our Lord Jesus has said, "No one can come to me unless the Father who sent me draws him" (Jn. 6:44).

1) It is the work of the Holy Spirit in men's hearts and souls that enables them to recognize Our Lord Jesus Christ and commit themselves to Him. No one can enter into friendship with God by his/her own power. This can only be done when God opens the way and gives the invitation. Yet we can pray and work so that others might receive this great gift of faith.

2) This light of faith dissipates the darkness of despair and death, and it and fills us with the hope of attaining eternal light and life. How grateful we should be for the precious gift of faith, for it enables us to possess Jesus Christ in our hearts and souls, and gives us the capacity to begin heaven even here on earth. Where Jesus Christ is, there is heaven.

****

1) That we frequently manifest our gratitude to Almighty God for the gift of faith, and that we continue to nourish it in our hearts and souls.

2) That we manifest our gratitude to Our Lord Jesus Christ for His Incarnation, and for His passion and death.

3) That we be ever conscious that our faith, like our intellects, is a light of varying degrees of intensity and that it must be continually nourished to grow.

4) For all of those men and women who have lost their faith, that God enkindle the light of faith within them; or for those who have grown cold or lukewarm, that God enkindle and enliven the light of faith within them.

5) That we continually pray that God's kingdom be extended here on earth.

January 2 (if a weekday): Jn. 1:19-28

I. St. John the Apostle was imbued with Jewish tradition. In chapter 16 of the Book of Deuteronomy, it is made clear that any important truth must be attested to by at least two credible witnesses.

1) In his Gospel, St. John the Apostle proclaims that Jesus is indeed the long-expected Messiah, and he uses John the Baptist as a reputable witness, one highly respected by the people, to bear witness to the identity of Jesus.

2) As a true prophet and servant of the Lord, John the Baptist did not try to seek his own aggrandizement or enhance his reputation in fulfilling his sacred mission of preparing the way of the Lord. Like a candle that spends itself in giving light, John the Baptist would spend himself preparing his people for the coming of the Messiah.

II. Jewish tradition held that Elijah was to come just before the Messiah was to make His presence known in the world. Even though John dressed like Elijah and possessed Elijah-like fire and zeal, he would not deceive his disciples nor the people by giving himself off as the famous prophet. Much less would he dare to pass himself off as the Messiah. Both of those roles he could easily have arrogated to himself. John was a lover of humility and truth; for this reason Christ loved him dearly.

III. Because John the Baptist was a son of a priest (Zechariah), he was therefore a descendant of the priestly house of Aaron; nevertheless, John's style of life, his message, and his ritual of baptism disturbed the Sanhedrin. One of the functions of the Sanhedrin was to verify the validity or authenticity of people who said that they were prophets. The delegation sent out to question John was commissioned by the Sanhedrin. Many of the members of the Sanhedrin were priests.

IV. John would not cower before this prestigious group. He merely answered the delegation honestly by way of a humble acknowledgment of the truth. He said that he was neither Elijah nor the Messiah. He said that he was preparing the way of the Lord, and that the Promised One had already arrived; he, John, did not consider himself worthy to loosen His sandal strap.

1) Loosening sandal straps was a chore reserved to slaves. Such was John's humility that he considered himself unworthy of occupying the position of a slave of the Messiah.

2) It was because of John's humility, courage, and love of truth that Jesus would say of him, "Of men born of women, there is none greater that John the Baptist" (Mt. 11:11).

V. Baptism is the initiation into and foundation of the life of God in the soul. It makes us sons and daughters of God the Father. Upon baptism, one's spiritual edifice is built. Baptism makes us Christians. It makes us totally committed to Christ. In the sacrament of confirmation we confirm what was spoken for us by our godparents in baptism. Many of the same questions that were put to our godparents are asked of us at confirmation; thus we literally confirm what was done for us at infant baptism. We recommit ourselves to Our Lord Jesus Christ.

1) St. Paul asks in his letter to the Romans: "Do you not know that all of us who have been baptized into Christ Jesus were baptized into his death?" He continues: "We were buried therefore with him, so that as Christ was raised from the dead by the glory of the Father, we too might walk in newness of life" (Rom. 6:3-5).

2) How fortunate we are to receive what John the Baptist himself did not receive — the baptism of Our Lord Jesus Christ! How grateful we should be!

3) Our baptismal day is our real birthday; St. Vincent Ferrer considered his baptismal day his birthday. With his heart full of gratitude, he used to have a stipend sent to the church of his baptism so that a Mass of thanksgiving might be offered in that church on that day. It was the day he was given eternal life.

4) When we think of our baptism, we should whisper a deep sigh

of gratitude because of the great dignity it confers on us. King St. Louis of France used to sign letters "Louis of Poissy." He said to a courtier, "In Poissy, I received the greatest honor of my life." "You mean, your majesty, in the city of Rheims." "No," the saintly king insisted. "It is true that in the city of Rheims I was consecrated a king on this earth, but at Poissy I was made a Christian. There I acquired a right to a throne in heaven" (A. Tonne, *Pastoral Life*).

VI. Through baptism we are incorporated into Christ and profess to lead a life modeled on the life of Our Lord Jesus Christ. Through baptism we profess to die to sin and lead a new life in Jesus Christ. Baptism makes us missionaries of the Gospel. It calls upon us to bear witness to the Gospel and to make its good news attractive to the unchurched.

****

1) That we frequently send up acts of gratitude for having received the gift of faith through our baptism.

2) That we come to realize more and more the great dignity and destiny baptism confers upon us.

3) That we pray for those who have betrayed their baptism through their failure to practice their faith.

4) That the Lord confer upon us a lively and prudent zeal for souls.

5) That we strive to become more conscious of the challenge baptism imposes upon us to grow in holiness and to spread the Good News of the Gospel of Our Lord Jesus Christ.

6) For all the souls in purgatory, especially for those who have no one to pray for them.

January 3 (if a weekday): Jn. 1:29-34

I. Once again John the Baptist makes it clear that his role was to reveal and identify the Messiah — the Promised and Anointed One of Israel's hopes and aspirations.

II. Perhaps one might remain a bit puzzled at John's statement, "I confess I did not recognize him, though the very reason I came baptizing with water was that he might be revealed to Israel." One might ask, if John was Jesus' cousin, how could it be that he did not recognize Him? What John clearly meant was that he did not recognize who Jesus really was, namely, the Messiah.

1) Jesus lived a quiet reclusive kind of a life for thirty years in Nazareth. John had no idea that his cousin was the Messiah. He no doubt recognized Jesus as his cousin, but hadn't the slightest idea that Jesus was the Messiah.

2) The same Holy Spirit that had sent John to baptize said to him, " 'When you see the Spirit descend and rest on someone, it is he who is to baptize with the Holy Spirit.' Now I have seen for myself and have testified: 'This is God's chosen One.' "

3) It was the Holy Spirit that gave John the light to recognize the Messiah. It is this same Holy Spirit who gives us the wherewithal to recognize Christ in other people.

III. John uses the phrase "Lamb of God" in pointing out Jesus as the Messiah to the people. This phrase speaks volumes in Jewish sacred history. The lamb was the animal selected most frequently to obtain the forgiveness of God for the sins of the people and of the entire Jewish nation, and this is basically what the role of the Messiah would be.

1) It was the blood of the paschal lamb sprinkled on the doorposts of the Jewish homes in Egypt that was to save the Jews from the avenging angel who came to strike down the firstborn of Egypt.

2) Every morning and evening a lamb would be sacrificed and offered on the altar of the temple as a sacrificial prayer pleading for pardon for the sins committed by the people.

3) John sees in Jesus the only One who can make reparation for the sins of the world. By employing the word "world," John is speaking prophetically under the influence of the Holy Spirit. He is not limiting Jesus' role exclusively to the Jews. On the contrary, Jesus was to take away the sins of all the world, Jew and Gentile alike.

IV. In the first reading, St. John the Apostle writes, "Dearly beloved, we are God's children now; what we shall later be has not yet come to light." Through baptism we become children of God. Baptism is the foundation of our life in God. We are called to be more and more like God through the sanctification of our souls. Baptism is the seed of Christianity; we must cooperate with God's grace to bring it to maturity and ultimately to Christian perfection so that people can recognize Christ dwelling in us.

1) In the early days of Christianity, pagans could recognize Christians through the genuine self-sacrificial love that Christians bore for one another. Charity is the virtue which should most reveal our identification with Christ. Charity more than any other virtue will draw people to Christ. Our Lord Jesus Christ has said, "By this shall all men know that you are my disciples, by the love you bear for one another" (Jn. 13:35).

2) We do more to reveal Christ to the world by the charity we practice in our daily lives. We bring Christ to others by the charity we implement in our daily living. If Christians really loved one another as Christ taught, the whole world would be Christian, for there is nothing more forceful and convincing than that selfless love that spends itself in service to others.

3) St. Paul tells us that we are temples of the Holy Spirit, that God really dwells in us. But it is up to us to make Christ manifest in us; to make Him come alive within us so that others might recognize His presence within us because of the seriousness with which we implement the Gospel in our daily lives. This we are called to do by our baptism and confirmation. This is the best evangelization we can possibly engage in. This is what makes people "see" Christ in the world.

****

1) That the Lord give us a deeper understanding of the sacraments of baptism and confirmation.

2) That we frequently express our gratitude to God for these sacraments.

3) That we realize that our faith is a gift of God and that to grow we must generously collaborate with the inspirations and graces of the Holy Spirit.

4) That we strive to implement the virtue of charity in our daily lives and really put ourselves out for others.

5) That we not harbor grudges and be generously forgiving of one another, especially forgiving of members of our families and relatives.

6) That we not be cold to those in need.

7) For the success of the ecumenical movement, that all Christians be one.

January 4 (if a weekday): Jn. 1:35-42

I. John the Baptist was indeed a humble man: his sentiments were always that Christ must increase and he must decrease. Before Jesus started His public ministry, John enjoyed prestige and fame. This was soon to diminish. He who had enjoyed the first place now most graciously accedes to take the lower place. John's obsession was to prepare the people to receive the Messiah, whom he, John, would point out. He was to show the people who the Messiah was, and he, John, would not be jealous of Him.

II. Today's Gospel shows us how some of John's disciples were leaving him to follow Jesus. John did not object to this; rather, he even encouraged it.

1) Andrew and John follow after Jesus at a distance. Realizing that they were following Him, Jesus turns around and asks them, "What are you looking for?" "Rabbi," they answered, "where are you staying?" "Come and see," Jesus replied.

2) Here we have an invitation to the interior life of intimacy with Our Lord Jesus Christ. All who seriously pursue Jesus will find Him, and they will receive that same invitation to divine intimacy.

III. St. Augustine wrote that God moves us by His grace to seek Him. This is the mystery of the prevenient grace of God. As St. John writes, "We love because he first loved us" (1 Jn. 4:19). We would not have the desire to seek God out unless God Himself first enkindled this desire within us.

1) This is the prevenient grace of God tugging at our heartstrings; it is an invitation to divine intimacy. God first loves us and then moves us to respond to that love.

2) Here we see something of the Prodigal Son, whose father never ceased loving him and would go out daily to the hilltop hoping to see his son returning.

IV. Jesus invites John and Andrew to spend the evening with Him. When they took their leave of Jesus, they were so filled with enthusiasm and joy that they had to tell their families and friends.

1) Andrew told his brother, Simon, that he and John spent time with the Messiah. Andrew brought his brother to see Jesus.

2) Like Andrew and John, once we have been introduced to Jesus and have spent time with Him, we too will become filled with a like enthusiasm to bring others to Him that they too might come to know Him, experiencing His love and His call to intimacy.

3) The invitation of Jesus is open to all of us. "Behold, I stand at the door and knock; if anyone hears my voice and opens the door, I will come in to him and eat with him, and he with me" (Rev. 3:20). He indicates that He knocks; this is His prevenient grace tugging at us, inviting us to divine intimacy. We must open the door of our hearts and spend time with Him in prayer and quiet solitude. If we do not attain intimacy with Our Lord Jesus Christ, it is because we are too busy to spend time alone with Him, talking and listening to the divine Guest of our souls.

4) Solitude is an absolute ingredient to divine intimacy. There is no reason why we cannot spend at least a half an hour alone with God where there is no intruding noise or distractions. In his Spiritual Canticle, St. John of the Cross, writing about the soul seeking intimacy with God, states, "She lived in solitude, and now in solitude has built her nest; and in solitude He guides her, He alone, who also bears in solitude the wound of love."

5) We are never wasting time when we are at prayer. St. John of the Cross tells us that we can do no greater work than expressing our sincere love of God in prayer. This is what wins for us that intimacy with Him who longs to share His love with us.

****

1) That God enkindle a desire for greater intimacy with Him within our hearts and souls.

2) That we cultivate a love for solitude, to be alone with God in meditative prayer.

3) That God fill us with a zeal for souls and for making Jesus known and loved by others.

4) That we be mindful to thank God for calling us to enjoy the gift of faith.

5) For the conversion of all of those who refuse to open the door of their hearts to Christ.

6) For the success of the ecumenical movement.

January 5 (if a weekday): Jn. 1:43-51

I. Ralph Waldo Emerson once said, "Nothing is more simple than greatness; indeed to be simple is to be great." What attracted Jesus to Nathanael (most probably Bartholomew) was his simplicity, his utter lack of guile or deceit. Simplicity is candor and utter lack of sophistication. It means being one's self as one is before God, in all honesty.

II. A fourteenth-century monk and philosopher by the name of William of Occam devised a principle that came to be known as "Occam's razor." It literally meant that principles should not be multiplied unnecessarily. This, in everyday language, means "cut the baloney and get to the heart of the matter." It means eliminating all that is superfluous. This is simplicity.

III. St. Francis of Assisi called simplicity the "sister of wisdom." He loved people endowed with this virtue. What pleased Francis in this virtue was the fear of the Lord that simplicity engenders. Its object is to please God in all that it does; it knows not how to do or speak evil. In his "Praises of Virtues," Francis writes, "Hail, Queen Wisdom! The Lord save you with your sister, pure, holy simplicity!"

IV. St. Francis had a special love for Brother John because he was richly endowed with simplicity. When John entered the order, he was so desirous of attaining perfection that he would imitate Francis in everything. If Francis would cough, John would cough; if Francis would sigh, so would John. When Francis would raise his arms in prayer, John would do likewise. Francis noticed this, and asked John why he was behaving in this way. The humble man said, "I have promised to do everything you do; it is dangerous for me to omit anything." Francis rejoiced because of John's simplicity, but gently forbade him from doing this in the future. Not long after, Brother John died. Francis often proposed him for imitation. With great joy, he called him, not Brother John, but St. John (Mark Steir, *Franciscan Life in Christ*).

V. "I saw you under the fig tree," Jesus said to Nathanael. Jesus was alluding to some event in Nathanael's life known only to Nathanael (Chautard). In his simplicity, Nathanael, deeply impressed, responds enthusiastically: "Rabbi, you are the Son of God. You are the king of Israel." Nathanael's quick act of faith is founded on the divine knowledge Jesus revealed in referring to the unknown event.

VI. Jesus assures Nathanael that he will see greater signs than the simple one Jesus revealed. "I solemnly assure you, you will see the sky opened and the angels of God ascending and descending on the Son of Man." Nathanael is promised a vision of heavenly things.

1) Jesus' reference to the angels ascending and descending refers to the account in Genesis 28:12, of the dream-vision Jacob had of angels ascending and descending on a ladder at Bethel.

2) Angels are messengers of God. In the Old Testament God used them to communicate His messages to people. In saying that the angels will ascend and descend on the Son of Man, Jesus is saying that He is the ladder between heaven and earth; His message is the final public communication of God to men. More messengers will not be needed.

VII. Like Nathanael, Jesus will communicate a deeper understanding and appreciation of His message to the upright and simple of heart, to those who really desire to know and love Him.

1) This simplicity of heart draws God to us and moves Him to communicate with us to infuse knowledge of divine things in us. Simplicity's priority is God; the Lord is its goal. Simplicity cuts away the superfluous and knows how to get to what really matters. For the genuinely simple of heart, what really matters is God. Because of this, God attends to the simple of heart.

2) Simplicity has that power of restoring innocence to the soul, to make it attractive to God again just as a child is attractive to an adult because of its innocence and lack of guile.

3) Nathanael possessed the simplicity that drew Jesus to him. It will draw God to us also, just as it will draw people to us. Simplicity puts people at ease because it makes us transparent to them and eliminates fear. Simplicity is a virtue we must work at by positively eliminating all guile and ulterior motives in our dealings with others and by making a positive effort to please God in all we do.

4) "Blessed are the pure of heart. . ." refers specifically to people who are blessed with this simplicity.

****

1) That we despise all deceitfulness in our daily lives.

2) That we strive to be open and honest with all with whom we live and work.

3) That we strive to free ourselves of ulterior motives in our dealings with others.

4) That husbands and wives be honest with each other and communicate openly in all aspects of their married lives.

5) That we consciously pray for this childlike virtue of simplicity.

6) Like Nathanael, that we too respond enthusiastically by praising God for His goodness to us, and that we give glory, honor, and praise to God for our successes.

January 6 (if a weekday): Mk. 1:7-11

I. John's baptism was a baptism of repentance. His baptism could not remit sins as the sacrament of baptism, instituted by Jesus, does. Nevertheless, for those who were sorry for their sins, the baptism of John was an external manifestation of their determination to cease committing sins in the future.

II. Jesus approved of John's baptism as an external profession of one's sorrow and detestation of sin. John knew that the Messiah's manifestation was imminent, as in today's Gospel he alerts the people whom he is baptizing: "One more powerful than I is coming after me. I am not fit to stoop and untie his sandal straps. I have baptized you in water; he will baptize in the Holy Spirit."

III. Shortly thereafter, Jesus does make His appearance at the Jordan where John was baptizing and asks to be baptized. Upon His reception of John's baptism, the heavens open, and God the Father proclaims Jesus as His Son. The Holy Spirit descends upon Him in the form of a dove, the sign that John was to receive to recognize the person of the Messiah. In acknowledgment that Jesus is the Messiah, the testimony of God the Father and God the Holy Spirit is given. This public testimony is immediately followed by John's proclamation: "Behold the lamb of God, who takes away the sin of the world" (Jn. 1:29).

1) In taking the form of a dove, the Holy Spirit reveals two of the self-evident characteristics that Jesus would naturally manifest to everyone: meekness, or gentleness, and peace. Jesus would impart that peace through meekness.

2) Jesus' message would not be one of threatening destruction or

90

of consuming fire that was so evident in John the Baptist's preaching. Jesus' message would be one of peace and love, while at the same time not losing any of the effectiveness of the supreme realities conveyed by His preaching — namely, the reality of heaven and hell, the necessity of bearing one's crosses in life, and the need to proceed along the narrow way to salvation. Unlike John with that forceful, stern style and stark appearance, Jesus would preach with a gentleness that was both moving and convincing. Unlike John, a recluse and an ascetic, Jesus would move about and mingle with the people, eating and drinking in their homes, even in the homes of chiselers, Pharisees, and sinners.

3) Like the dove, Jesus would attract the people through His gentleness, compassion, and loving forgiveness.

IV. With the baptism of John, Jesus formally began His public ministry. His hour had come to declare Himself after thirty years of solitude. With John's baptism, Jesus started on the road that would lead to His crucifixion and death. Clinging to the meekness and gentleness with which He began His ministry, Jesus would lay down His life with the same meekness and gentleness.

V. Jesus tells us, "Learn of me for I am meek and humble of heart" (Mt. 11:29). "Nothing is so strong as gentleness," says St. Francis de Sales, "and nothing is gentle as real strength." Of this, Jesus is the paragon.

1) When Yahweh revealed Himself to Elijah, it wasn't in a mighty wind, an earthquake, or in fire; rather it was in a gentle breeze (3 Kgs. 19:11-12). As a father, God is gentle with us, so we should be gentle in our treatment of others, always recognizing their dignity as sons and daughters of God.

2) More flies are caught with a drop of honey than a barrel of vinegar (St. Francis de Sales). If we are to be effective in our apostolate, gentleness must pervade our style. Gentleness is the enemy of arrogance, which is a manifestation of pride. One's natural reaction is to resist the proud.

3) Gentleness muzzles our irascible appetite and subdues outbursts of anger. It makes us approachable to people. We really grow in strength when we grow in gentleness. Gentleness makes us Christlike. It is an excellent tool in evangelization, for it draws and

attracts people to the source of that gentleness, which is Our Lord Jesus Christ Himself.

****

1) That we make a conscious effort to curb our anger.

2) That we not retort at an insult, but offer it to God as a salutary penance in imitation of our Savior who bore insult and injury.

3) That we strive to be gentle in dealing with others, especially with the members of our families.

4) That husbands and wives treat each other with meekness and gentleness and refrain from all harshness and meanness.

5) That we strive to bend the meanness and crossness of others with gentleness.

6) That the Lord give us the strength to persevere in gentleness and meekness in all of our undertakings.

January 7 (if a weekday): Jn. 2:1-12

I. St. John notes that there were six stone water jars standing at the entrance of the house at Cana, and they were used for the ceremonial washings before entering the house. Jesus orders them to be filled with water to be changed into perfect wine.

1) Six is a number in Jewish tradition which signified imperfection. Judaism itself was incomplete until the coming of the Messiah, who would fulfill the prophecies and bring about man's redemption; thus Christ would bring the Old Testament to perfection with the proclamation of His Gospel and the establishment of His kingdom on earth.

2) Together with bread, Jesus would later select wine to be the basic matter of every Eucharistic Banquet. At every Mass, Jesus changes wine into His Body and Blood so as to give us life and life in abundance.

II. St. John tells us that this was the first of the signs wherein the glory of Jesus was revealed, and His disciples believed in Him. John only records seven of Jesus' miracles. John was the last of the Evangelists to write his Gospel. His purpose in writing it was as he himself states in chapter 20, verse 31: "That you may believe that Jesus is the Christ, the Son of God, and that believing, you may have life in his name."

1) John is selective of the miracles of Jesus, and he narrates them so that they might reveal the glory of Jesus and convince his readers that Jesus is indeed the Christ, that belief in Him will bring life.

2) To John was consigned the Blessed Virgin Mary, a living source of knowledge concerning Jesus, which gave the beloved disciple an eagle's-eye view of the events and the meaning of those events in the life of Our Lord Jesus Christ.

3) John saw no need of narrating any more of Jesus' miracles, since the other three Evangelists had already given sufficient testimony of them in their Gospels.

III. Mary gave Jesus His Body and Blood in her womb. It is through her, therefore, that this precious, life-giving Flesh and Blood is given to us. Mary is the bridge between God and mankind. St. Augustine said of her, "All the elect while they are on this earth are hidden in the womb of the most holy Virgin that they may be made more like the image of the Son of God. There they are protected, formed, and sustained by this loving mother."

1) St. Ambrose writing in a similar vein states, "O God, You who made all things, created Mary: He who created everything from nothing did not will to remake a fallen world except through Mary."

IV. It is because of Mary that Jesus worked the miracle, for He clearly indicated that His hour had not yet come. This clearly shows the intercessory power of the Blessed Virgin Mary.

1) It is John's Gospel that reveals that Jesus gave Mary to us to be our mother. Mary passed through the gamut of human suffering, and can identify with all her suffering and hurting sons and daughters.

2) In the East, hospitality was a sacred duty. It would have been a painfully embarrassing thing for the hosts of a banquet to have their guests go without wine, for wine simply was a necessary part of the celebration. It was to save embarrassment to the young married couple that Mary interceded and asked her Son to do something. Even though Jesus did not want to work any miracles at that time, nevertheless He accedes to the urgings of His mother.

3) St. Louis de Montfort said, "I do not believe that anyone could achieve an intense union with God and perfect fidelity with the Holy Spirit unless one has established a profound union with the Blessed Virgin" (St. Louis-Marie de Montfort, *True Devotion to the Blessed Virgin*).

4) Since Jesus came into this world through Mary, it seems logical that we go to Jesus through Mary.

****

1) That we frequently fly to Mary and beg her to intercede for us before the throne of her Son.

2) That we too be sensitive and compassionate to others in their needs and help them avoid embarrassment.

3) That all young people preparing for marriage take seriously their commitment to their vows.

4) That all couples having difficulties in their marriages go to Mary for help and inspiration.

5) That through the intercession of the Blessed Virgin Mary, those who are experiencing doubts in their faith be affirmed in it.

6) For all those who are sincerely seeking a suitable person to marry, that they may find an ideal companion.

7) For peace in the world and an end to terrorism.

Monday after Epiphany: Mt. 4:12—17:23-25

I. When John the Baptist was imprisoned in the castle of Machaerus by King Herod Antipas for denouncing Herod for the crime of incest, Jesus withdrew to the province of Galilee to the town of Capernaum.

II. Because of its fertility, Galilee was a heavily populated province. Josephus, the Jewish historian, states that there were some 204 villages in Galilee, each with a population of at least 15,000 (W. Barclay, *Gospel of Matthew*). Jesus actually begins His public ministry of preaching, teaching, and healing in this heavily populated province. He continues the same keynote of John's preaching: repentance and conversion to God and the things of God.

III. Jesus uses the synagogues for His forum. The people who cared to hear the Scriptures read and expounded upon would come to the synagogues. These synagogues gave Jesus an excellent opportunity to preach and instruct. Although there was only one temple in Israel where animals were offered in sacrifice, there were many synagogues throughout the country, but the sacrifices of animals were not permitted in them. This could only take place in the temple. This temple, located in Jerusalem, was the only temple in the entire country. It was, naturally, the heart and soul of Jewish national worship.

IV. People came from all over Galilee and beyond, from the Decapolis east of the Jordan River. Many people came even from the Diaspora (those living outside of Palestine). By passing through the Decapolis where He cured the deaf man (Mk. 7:31), early on in His ministry, Jesus indicated that His Gospel was also for the Gentiles, since the Decapolis was Hellenistic or Greek, inhabited mostly by Gentiles. The Decapolis referred to the ten cities located in eastern Palestine which came under the jurisdiction of the Roman legate of Syria. It was a territory that extended from Damascus in the North (which is in Syria) to Philadelphia in southeastern Palestine, east of Peraea (McKenzie, *Dictionary of the Bible*). As Jesus' fame grew, people with all kinds of sicknesses were being brought to Him: the lame, the paralyzed, the possessed, etc.; Jesus healed them all.

V. Jesus instructed, enlightened, and healed wherever He went. He announced the reign of God was at hand, and that in order to receive and accept it, one had to repent sincerely of his/her sins.

1) Repentance is a true detestation for sin, a sorrow for having offended God, and a turning toward Him for pardon and mercy.

2) Repentance demands an acknowledgment for having offended God, a confession of one's guilt, and a manifestation of sorrow. God will never refuse a humble and contrite heart. Repentance lasts as long as life itself. It is a turning from sin to God, and this must be a permanent, ongoing attitude of mind and soul. Repentance is a habitual attitude of soul which perseveres in a lasting sorrow for having offended God.

3) Jesus' instruction and preaching did little to illuminate the hardhearted. Sincere contrition is necessary for the darkness to be lifted from our minds and for the light of faith to enter in there. Where sin kills, repentance imparts life and light.

VI. Once we are forgiven, God "forgets" our sins, and He will never hold them over us. He returns to the soul to dwell there. Repentance draws God into the soul.

1) Before Jesus would extend His hand to cure or heal physical illnesses or afflictions, He always expected, as preliminary requisites, sorrow for having offended God and faith and confidence in Him in His power to heal both soul and body.

2) Cardinal Cushing once said, "No one is a born Catholic; we are all converts." As we grow older, we must continually recommit ourselves. Saints are people who have experienced healing the most. Their repentance was keen, deep, and permanent. Thomas Merton wrote, "The lives of those who have been truly close to God have taught us that the saints are the ones who more than all others have felt in themselves the evil of sin and the need of pardon."

3) Without doubt, repentance stands at the forefront of the important doctrines of the New Testament. Jesus began His public ministry preaching repentance. Happiness and peace can only come through true sorrow for our sins. On this sorrow we build our relationship with God.

****

1) That God give us a sincere and abiding sorrow for having offended Him.

2) That we frequently ask God to pardon our sins and those of our family.

3) Since many in today's world have lost their sense of sin, that God may quicken their consciences so that they may recognize the seriousness of their plight.

4) That we constantly strive to make reparation for our sins, especially through prayer, the rosary, and acts of charity toward our neighbor.

5) Charity covers a multitude of sins, and one of the arms of charity is almsgiving; that we be generous to those in need as an expression of our genuine sorrow and reparation.

6) For reconciliation among the nations of the world with one another.

Tuesday after Epiphany: Mk. 6:34-44

I. It is interesting to note that this is the only miracle that is recorded by all of the Evangelists, Matthew, Mark, Luke, and John. It could be so because they were so overwhelmed by the awesomeness of this outstanding episode, or because it was a logical preparation for an instruction on the Eucharist, the Bread of Life.

II. Mark records that there were twelve baskets of leftovers. We know there were twelve Apostles who were being formed by Christ for the ministry of the Eucharist. In today's Gospel episode, Christ tells His Apostles to distribute the loaves and fishes to the hungry masses.

1) The Apostles were going to be the real instruments for bringing the life-giving Eucharist to the world. They were to go out later to establish the Church throughout the world, to ordain other bishops and priests to make the multiplication of Christ's Body a reality to the communities and masses of people whom they would one day evangelize.

2) The Apostles and their successors were going to be Christ's instruments for confecting this marvelous sacrament — the real manna come down from heaven, the Body and Blood of Our Lord Jesus Christ, and distribute it to the spiritually hungry masses.

III. The Apostles notice that the hour is getting late and that hunger is overtaking the people. They appeal to Our Lord. Jesus throws the responsibility back on to them: "You give them something to eat."

1) We cannot be buck passers; individually each one of us has a responsibility toward our less fortunate brothers and sisters.

2) It is true that in today's Gospel the task was beyond their reach. When Our Lord said, "You give them something to eat," He meant doing the little you can to relieve the want of others. Every little bit helps. Charity obliges us to do what we reasonably can, and God will do the rest by multiplying our efforts. When in a community all do their part, the poor will be fed. God will use our humble efforts to move others to do their bit. Charity simply is catching.

IV. All God wants is a responsive and generous heart that will offer itself to do what it can, and He will do the rest. In a similar manner, Christ's passion and death won God's forgiveness for all of man's sins; nevertheless, Christ wills that we too contribute our share to His sufferings and death for the ongoing work involved in the sanctification and salvation of souls, as St. Paul writes in his letter to the Colossians: ". . . And what is lacking of the sufferings of Christ, I fill up in my flesh for his body which is the church" (Col. 1:24).

1) God always uses human instruments to do His great and

magnificent works. Through people like Mother Teresa and Dorothy Day, thousands of people are fed and given hospitality.

2) As individuals, we cannot feed the world, but we can subscribe to organizations that have as their goals the feeding of the hungry masses. Organizations like the U.S. Catholic Relief Service, Bread for the World, the Salvation Army, UNICEF, etc. As individuals, we are quite helpless to alleviate the hunger of the masses. With organized groups, thousands can be recipients of our aid.

V. All of us are given talents of one kind or another. God does expect us to use them. However meager these talents may seem to be, He can do marvels with them. In God's hands they can be transformed. We are our brothers' and sisters' keepers, even of those we do not see in far-off lands. They still ask for our help. Television has made this world a smaller place. It can make the needs of our brothers and sisters in far-off lands known to us. God wills to help them through us, the other members of His Body. We then become, like the Apostles, so many extensions of Christ's hands in feeding the hungry.

****

1) That our devotion to Our Lord Jesus Christ in the Eucharist grow.

2) That we visit Our Lord in the Blessed Sacrament frequently to pray silently to Him who is truly present in the tabernacle.

3) That we learn to develop our talents and put them to use to help others.

4) That we do our best to alleviate world hunger.

5) That we warmly respond to those in need with our time, our resources, and our talents.

6) That governments of well-off countries do more to help the hungry of today's world.

Wednesday after Epiphany: Mk. 6:45-52

I. The victory over the waters is an important theme in Jewish cosmogony. Cosmogony is the science that studies the evolution of the universe. The Bible describes the creation of the earth as a victory by God over the sea and the evil monsters it was believed to shelter. Later on in biblical history came the victory of God over the Red Sea to save His chosen people from the pursuing Egyptians. Today's Gospel narrates the victory of Jesus over the stormy lake. The early Christians interpreted the stilling of the tempest and the walking on the waters as manifestations of Him who was bringing the work of creation to fulfillment (Maertens and Frisque).

II. Just as Moses led the chosen people across the Red Sea, Jesus, the new Moses, leads the Apostles through the stormy waters safely to shore.

1) Christ's walking on the waters is an affirmation that He has overcome the power of evil. Prior to His coming, all creation was imprisoned by sin, shackled under the power of Satan and his minions. Our Lord Jesus Christ broke the bonds of Satan and of sin.

2) The miracle of Jesus walking upon the waters symbolizes His power over the devil and over all evil. The sea in the Semitic mind symbolized all evil, since it was believed to harbor killer monsters who were thought capable of even crushing ships. This was in fact one of the real fears of Christopher Columbus's crew on their voyage west to the New World.

III. When St. Augustine commented on the pericope of Jesus walking upon the rough waters of the Sea of Galilee, he wrote, "He came treading the waves, and so He puts all the swelling tumults of life under His feet. Christians — why afraid?" (cited in W. Barclay). "The only thing we have to fear," said Franklin Delano Roosevelt in his first inaugural address, "is fear itself."

1) Fear is a great obstacle to love, and love is the only key to intimate union with God. There is a constant interplay between these two forces in the life of every human being. Love, however, begets trust, and the lover learns to trust even blindly in his/her Beloved, who, for the Christian, is Our Lord Jesus Christ Himself dwelling in his/her soul.

2) Where Christ is, there the storm abates and becomes calm, the tumult subsides, and the threats of danger and feelings of anxiety subside.

3) When Pope Paul VI entered the office of his predecessor for the first time after his elevation to the papacy, he sat down at the desk and put his head into his hands at the sight of the magnitude of the problems that faced him. Tears came to his eyes. Feeling

thoroughly overcome by it all, he had a deep sense of inability to cope with all these problems. Then his eye caught sight of a holy card with the picture of Christ calming the stormy seas. He immediately picked up courage, for there and then he knew that Christ Himself was with him and would help and guide him, His vicar on earth, through any storm.

IV. To walk with Our Lord is to conquer the storms that arise at times in our lives and threaten to engulf us. To walk with Jesus Christ means to cultivate a sense of the presence of God in our souls and to be frequently conscious of His divine presence.

1) Some people manage to do this by making frequent ejaculatory prayers and by intermittently offering their work during the day to God.

2) St. Teresa of Ávila told one of her nuns who complained that she wasn't getting enough time for prayer. "Run along, my daughter, the Lord walks among the pots and pans."

3) Brother Lawrence spent much of his working life in the monastery kitchen amid dirty dishes. He said, "I felt Jesus Christ close to me in the kitchen as ever I did before the Blessed Sacrament."

4) As a young girl, St. Catherine of Siena complained to Our Lord that she wasn't permitted to get to church as often as she would like. The Lord told her to make a sanctuary in her heart; there He would visit her as often as she liked.

5) We must all learn to reach into the sanctuary of our hearts and souls to find Our Lord Jesus, so that in times of crisis or in the darkness of doubts we might more readily find Him there to calm our troubled waters.

****

1) Love casts out fear; that God may intensify our love for Him.

2) In our times of apprehension and worry, that we resort to prayer and reflect meditatively on the Scriptures.

3) That we always be sensitive to others caught in the grip of fear and anxiety, and strive to help them to alleviate their plight.

4) For parents apprehensive about their children because of the dangers that confront them, especially in the areas of drugs,

promiscuity, and pornography, that they commit the children to the Lord who gave them to them as their sacred charges.

5) For the elderly and the lonely, that they strive to cultivate a sensitivity to the presence of God within them.

6) That we all learn to have recourse to Sacred Scripture, especially to the pages of the New Testament when we feel inundated with the troubled waters of our problems.

7) For peace in the world and an end to terrorism.

Thursday after Epiphany: Lk. 4:14-22

I. Jesus' fame was growing because of the authority with which He spoke and the miracles He was working. He was a welcome guest in the synagogues around Israel until He claimed to fulfill Isaiah's prophecy in the synagogue of Nazareth, the claim which is narrated in today's Gospel.

1) When Jesus entered a synagogue, He would invariably be asked to read and comment on the Scriptures. Jesus would use the invitation as an opportunity to spread His Gospel.

2) Now He was in His own hometown of Nazareth, where He had been known from childhood. Here too He was invited to take up the scrolls of Sacred Scripture, and Jesus selected His reading from the passage of Isaiah referring to the Messiah (Is. 61:1-2).

3) Jesus announces that Isaiah's prophecy was being fulfilled in their very midst. In so many words He was saying that He was the Messiah — the One who was to come to bring glad tidings to the poor, to give sight to the blind, and to set captives free (that is, all those who were in the captivity of Satan and sin). The kingdom of God was in their midst, and Jesus was inaugurating it.

II. The neighbors and kinsmen of Jesus could not believe what they were hearing. They knew that he was Joseph the carpenter's son, and that He had no formal education.

1) Those who knew Him since His childhood figured that He had either lost His mind or, worse, that He was guilty of blasphemy.

2) Enraged, the crowd rose up and seized Him, taking Him to the brow of a steep hill on which the town was built. In compliance with the Mosaic Law, which called for death to one who blasphemed, they were going to hurl Him to His death. Whereupon Jesus miraculously slipped out of their midst.

III. The inhabitants were blinded and limited by the plain, simple atmosphere in which Jesus, like themselves, lived and had been raised. In their indignation, they had completely forgotten about all the miracles He had been working around Israel.

1) Their prejudice would not allow them to permit Jesus to prove Himself, nor to listen to His message. How often we, like the people in that synagogue in Nazareth, have similar tendencies to criticize people and put them into airtight boxes in our minds. We too don't give some people the opportunity to prove themselves by allowing them time to see how they act and react among people in the give-and-take of daily living and working. Charity demands that we let people have the opportunity to grow and develop.

2) God often sends His messages through the instrumentality of other people, and because of the plainness of these people or their background, we do not always accept their message. This was so with the Jews in regard to the prophets. Prophets were often rejected and persecuted because they prophesied chastisements to be meted out to the people or their leaders. Prophets pointed out their immoral living and refusal to do penance or live up to their commitments to Yahweh, their God.

3) We all want to hear pleasant things, but these pleasant things may not be beneficial to us spiritually. If they are not what we want to hear, it is so easy to close our ears to such messages.

IV. Today's Gospel is a plea for openness, openness to God's message, which constantly challenges us to follow Our Lord Jesus Christ and to stop adjusting or accommodating His message to meet our convenience.

1) The Gospel challenges us not to judge others, because God is the only One who really knows all the facts necessary to make an objective judgment on a person.

2) The Gospel challenges us not to water down our commitment to follow Christ along the narrow road to perfection. It challenges us to be open to God's message to us, no matter how or through whom it may come, or what it actually asks of us. Once we are certain it is the will of God, let us act on it even though it may cost us to do so.

****

1) That we be ever open to God's word and message for us.

2) That we respond to the inspirations of the Holy Spirit and grow in faith.

3) That we strive to tear down all barriers of prejudice, especially toward other people.

4) That we never keep grudges or harbor vengeful thoughts.

5) That our desire to know more about our faith grow and that our taste for God's word in Sacred Scripture increase and become more refined.

6) That we generously accept fraternal corrections and always be open to truth.

7) For all victims of prejudice and coldheartedness, that they may find solace in the word of God and peacefully continue to work for justice.

Friday after Epiphany: Lk. 5:12-16

I. In Leviticus 13:45, we read: "A man infected with leprosy must wear his clothing torn and his hair disordered; he must shield his beard and cry, 'unclean, unclean.' As long as the disease lasts he must be unclean, and therefore live apart: he must live outside of the camp."

1) It was absolutely forbidden for a leper to come near a healthy person, especially a Jew. When Jesus touched this leper, He violated the Mosaic Law, a thing He would always do in the face of human need.

2) The cleansing and healing of lepers was one of the signs of the presence of the Messiah. When some of the disciples of John the Baptist came to Jesus to ascertain if Jesus was the Messiah, Jesus answered by saying, "Go back and tell John what you hear and see, the blind see again, the lame walk, and lepers are cleansed. . ." (Mt. 11:4-5).

II. We can imagine the lot of lepers in Jewish society. They must have been a very depressed and forlorn people. They were considered unclean and therefore were prohibited from entering into the temple to participate in the worship of the community. They were literally outcasts, pariahs, shut off from contact with members of their own families. They were considered dead.

1) Lepers' lot was a living death, and death was their only

escape. No doubt many were driven to suicide. Anything that held out a glimmer of hope for a cure was most welcome news to them.

2) The leper of today's Gospel story heard of Jesus of Nazareth, the miracle worker. When the leper heard that Jesus was in the area, he was filled with enthusiasm and hope. In spite of the fact that the Mosaic Law prohibited lepers from coming anywhere near healthy people, nothing was going to stop him from getting access to Jesus. He approached Jesus and threw himself at the Savior's feet, crying out, "Lord, if you will to do so, you can cure me."

3) Jesus' response was immediate, and in His compassion He ignored the Mosaic Laws regarding touching lepers. Touching, He restored the leper to full health.

III. Leprosy is the closest physical counterpart to sin, for what leprosy does to the human body sin does to the soul. Sin is like a leprosy of the soul, driving God's grace out and eating away at the soul, ultimately bringing about its eternal death.

1) Unlike the effects of physical leprosy, we cannot see the damage and corrosion that sin causes in the soul. God can see our souls, and sin makes us leprous to His eyes. Just as leprosy excluded the lepers from society and made them outcasts, sin does this to a person also: it excludes him/her from active union with the Church, which is the Mystical Body of Christ. Such a one becomes a cancerous or leprous member and is cut off from receiving the life-communicating elements of God's vivifying grace.

2) Temptation is always attractive on the surface and tends to blind us as to the consequences it brings to our souls.

3) Stealing and cheating may present themselves as a means needed for security. Adultery and fornication offer seductive pleasures. Even murder can present itself as a promise of peace by eliminating an enemy or troublemaker. Temptations have their appealing charm and seductiveness, but they have an inevitable time-bomb effect in their package.

4) The devil seeks to make us rationalize our consciences. Lust is justified in the name of psychological growth or the need for the personal expression of one's affection and love for another. Anger is coated over to satisfy one's "just" indignation. Much is done in the name of the "good life" and the need of filling out the third dimension of one's personality. So it goes for alcohol and drug

taking. At the bottom of many lawsuits are pure covetousness and greed, which seek settlements far beyond the damages sustained.

IV. We must learn to flee sin, especially grave sin, as we would flee from the occasion of contracting leprosy or AIDS. When the Empress Eudoxia consulted with her courtiers on ways of revenging herself on John Chrysostom, the bishop of Constantinople, they told her that no physical pain would hurt him because he would see it as a chance to suffer for God. "If you really want to avenge him," they said, "there is only one way: you must get him to sin. Sin is the only thing he fears." It should really be the only thing we must fear.

****

1) That we may have a realistic knowledge of sin and a strong hatred of it.

2) That we cultivate a devotion to our guardian angels, who alert us to the activity of the devil and his proximity to us.

3) Since Our Lord Jesus Christ tells us to pray always lest we fall into temptation, that we may grow in our prayerfulness.

4) Because the only way to cleanse the leprosy of sin is through penance and reconciliation, that we never linger in serious sin, but rather have quick recourse to the sacrament of penance and reconciliation.

5) Through the intercession of the Blessed Virgin Mary, that we all be preserved from a sudden and unprovided death.

Saturday after Epiphany: Jn. 3:22-30

I. Today's Gospel demonstrates the humility, courage, and truth of St. John the Baptist. His popularity was such that he could have arrogated to himself the title of "Messiah." When the shift of popularity went from him to Jesus, John rejoiced. He refers to Jesus as the Groom at the wedding upon whom attention should be focused; he, John, is content and rejoices at being the best man.

1) The prophets frequently resorted to the imagery of Israel being the bride of God. Now John, the last and the greatest of the prophets, refers to Jesus as being the Groom, the Groom of Israel, His bride. John rejoices that at last the Messiah has come to save the people from their sins.

2) John's joy was to hear His voice, the voice of the

long-expected Messiah. "That is my joy, and it is complete. He must increase while I must decrease."

II. Humility and truth are sister virtues. Humility is a manifestation of truth, the truth of oneself. It also involves courage to practice humility, since we are naturally prone to pride and self-love. Truth can be embarrassing and humiliating.

1) John the Baptist was not trying to be more or less than what he really was. He refused to allow the people to entertain false and grandiose impressions about him.

2) John's greatness lies in his humility. Humility is the necessary ingredient for generous service, and service is the test of humility, especially when the people we serve are below our social level or station. John was first and foremost a servant of God.

3) When great deeds are analyzed, behind all the great men and women responsible for them stands the One who selected them and gave them the wherewithal to do them, to bring them to a happy conclusion. This person is God, who invariably takes the humble position behind the scenes, waiting for His servants to give Him that recognition that is due Him. All too often credit is focused on human beings rather than on the true source, the One who made the accomplishment of such great things possible — God Himself.

III. The word "humility" comes from the Latin root "humus," meaning "earth" or "ground."

1) The Lord has told us to learn of Him because He is humble of heart; that to become great in God's eyes we must learn to take the lowly places that are not fraught with distinction and recognition; and finally not seek to be served but to serve.

2) It has been said that the gates of heaven are so low that one must enter on one's knees. It is the humble that God exalts.

3) At the age of nineteen, St. Francis de Sales fell seriously ill. He called his favorite teacher and said to him, "Arrange my funeral but leave my body for the medical students. It is very consoling to me as I lie dying to think that while I was a useless servant in life, I will at least serve some good after death."

4) Such is our pride and self-love that St. Teresa of Jesus, a Doctor of the Church, once remarked, "A vision from the devil would do a humble person no harm; whereas a vision from God to a proud person would do no good."